I0439327

Our Life with Bigfoot

Knowing our Next of Kin at Habituation Sites

Christopher Noël

Also by Christopher Noël

How Sasquatch Matters: Writers Respond to the New Natural Order
Sasquatch Rising 2013: How DNA Breakthroughs and Backyard Visits Reveal the Greatest story of Our Time
Doctor White's Monkey (stories)
In the Unlikely Event of a Water Landing: A Georgraphy of Grief (memoir)
Hazard and the Five Delights (novel)

Table of Contents

Preface

This is serious. While most Sasquatch can take care of themselves—or else they would not have survived alongside our own species for thousands of years—others are vulnerable to great harm. As this book will make clear, these creatures occasionally engage in certain consistent routines at places where they feel safe, where they have come to trust our peaceful intentions.

But this trust can also expose them to grave danger, diminishing their age-old defenses of stealth, avoidance, and deeply entrenched fear.

Just last week, for example, self-proclaimed "master Bigfoot tracker" Rick Dyer found his way to a very active habituation site in East Texas, the last one featured here (Texas #2: pages 89-119). He did not, of course, learn of its location from me, but determined killers have their methods.

Much as I would love to tell what happened next on this property, the story is not mine to share; suffice it to say that on the first night, Sasquatch were seen and shots were fired.

I have spent many fascinating days and nights at this place, becoming friends with the person who lives there and learning the nature and behavior of the giants who sometimes visit her. To have it suddenly violated by someone with a bloodthirsty agenda and no goal other than self-aggrandizement makes me sick, as it does many others. This is why we need to organize an all-out effort to enact national protective legislation.

Rick Dyer at Texas #2 habituation site, February 2014, armed with a 30.06 rifle

But let me be absolutely clear: The campaign on behalf of Sasquatch does not single out any one individual; Rick Dyer merely *represents* a militant, ego-driven worldview that is unfortunately quite widespread:

> "Every Bigfoot should be hunted down and killed. Protection…my ass. We need to make 'em extinct. People, you should find a weapon, get out in the woods…you want to shoot 'em in the head, shoot 'em in the back of the neck, make 'em go down quick. If Christopher Noël tries to get you to communicate with Bigfoot, he's trying to kill you, and the blood is going to be on his hands! Bigfoot is a Monster!" (From YouTube: "Let's Make Bigfoot Extinct!")

Whether or not you believe that this man shot and killed a Sasquatch in the woods outside of San Antonio on September 6, 2012, you can witness his naked desperation to do so in the final night scene of the documentary "Shooting Bigfoot." (See my

YouTube video: "'Shooting Bigfoot' Shows Real Sasquatches.") If he did not succeed, he has nonetheless become a high-profile figure, a lightning rod for others who would love nothing more than to achieve his level of fame and notoriety. Many who understand that Sasquatch exists, but believe that Dyer is hoaxing his specimen, are already in the forests with night-vision technology and high-powered rifles, intending to do for real what Dyer has only pretended to do. If we see an authentic San Antonio specimen (not to be confused with the mere "replica" Dyer has taken on tour), this news will only serve to add fuel to the fire, leading quickly to a conflagration. If not, the next corpse will soon emerge, this time for real.

Even today, dozens of men on this continent are on the hunt, convinced that their very own million-dollar trophy awaits them among the trees; and they are not wrong. To take just one more example, Justin Smeja, star of the documentary "Dead Bigfoot" (www.deadbigfoot.com), claims that in October of 2010, he shot and killed a very young Sasquatch, and also shot an adult, which got away.

In his newly released book, *Sasquatch for Sale,* Michael Greene reports that this man, too, is hell bent for personal glory.

> Eager to prove his truthfulness, Justin has begun to spend all his free time (which can be considerable when you are self-employed) in the Sierras, now armed with a .300 Winchester Magnum rifle. This caliber is a favorite among North American big game hunters, with a typical 180-grain bullet (almost twice the weight of those used in Justin's old .25-06), travelling over 3000 feet per second. Just the ticket if you ever get the chance to shoot another. On the Spike TV show ["Million Dollar Bigfoot Bounty"], Justin made the statement that he didn't plan to spend the next twenty years trying to prove they exist—just shoot one and be done with it.

(Indicentally, for those who watched the 2013 British Channel 4 docmentary “Bigfoot: The New Evidence,” later rebroadcast on the National Geographic Channel, Smeja’s story was willfully misrepresented there. In the series’ dramatic conclusion, geneticist Bryan Sykes *seemed* to shatter Smeja’s account of the shooting, when in fact this is patently false. Greene clearly lays out the elements of this misrepresentation at the end of *Sasquatch for Sale.*)

If these two men are currently highly visible in the public eye as hell bent on “bringing in” a Sasquatch, think how many others are quietly going about the job in private, beneath the radar, not distracting themselves with premature media attention. Moreover, this number will immediately swell to thousands once the Dyer body is verified by science or another specimen is bagged and hauled in before the media. One of the two events is inevitable and not far off; if we wait passively until afterward to begin to mobilize against further slaughter, further slaughter will occur before it can be stopped.

And I won’t be the least bit surprised when, in addition to the “solo male warior” model, we then find women and children, too, going out with Dad to hunt Sasquatch for sport, for a grand, redemptive payday, just as they would play the lottery, except that *this* is a game the whole family can play and is a far more primordial thrill—us against the Monster. And the beast will stand in for poverty, obscurity, a lifetime of bum luck, or for whatever lousy hand these folks feel they have been dealt by the world.

Of course, television shows are hurrying to jump on the bandwagon as well.

Nor will the array of hunters be bothered by any pesky moral considerations, thanks to the culturally dominant viewpoint ringing in their ears, the one that gives Mankind dominion over all the earth.

This book is meant to directly counter this prevailing viewpoint, shining a light on profound kinship reather than hierarchy. In the pages that follow, pay special attention to the striking commonalities among the habituation experiences. And keep in mind that at the time the people involved did not know each other and lived, in some cases, thousands of miles apart. In other words, they were *independently* encountering the same phenomena. Back in 2008, when I started to connect with habituators and received their permission to gather together their careful, extensive testimonials, only a very few Sasquatch behaviors had yet been made public through books and television shows: tree-peeking, wood knocking, howls, whoops, and the leaving of footprints. A far richer, stranger, and more compelling suite of communicative overtures revealed itself to me as I learned from these residents and also began to witness for myself some of the events they have chronicled.

- Gift and food exchanges
- Window peeking
- "Borrowing" and later return of household/yard items
- Object manipulation and rearrangement
- Mimicry of human voices and animal sounds
- Subtle percussions such as tapping or scratching

on windows/exterior walls

- Non-subtle percussions such a slapping or banging on the side of the house or an outbuilding
- Muffled but palpable "thumps" on the ground, apparently produced at a distance but felt as a low-frequency vibration traveling through the turf to the human perceiver
- Sounds of spoken language, variously described as “chatter,” Russian, Chinese, or human speech rapidly played *backward*
- The appearance of stick and tree structures in the yard or nearby woods—arrangements that are obviously not randomly/ naturally occurring
- The breaking of branches or whole thick tree limbs at night—can be quiet or extremely loud
- Several colors of eye-glow—*not* reflected light—including red, amber, yellow, green
- Throwing or tossing of pebbles, rocks, sticks, clumps of mud/dirt
- “Spying” on residents from the edge of the forest or from behind outbuildings/ bushes/other obstructions

The vast majority of Sasquatch activity at such locations falls into the category of playful mischief. Why? Consider, first, that these visitors have brains at least twice the size of ours and, second, that they are fellow members of the genus *Homo*. This means that they are nothing less than *another species of human*, yet they do not use those massive brains to write books or symphonies, to build cities or machines or universities. Instead, they hunt for food and hang around in the woods with plenty of time on their hands and a natural primate thirst for stimulation, for engagement with their equals—with *us*. Thus, they feel a kindred tug, a curiosity born of ancient bonds of blood. They'll attempt to catch our attention, to "get a rise out of us," to see if we will wake up and join the game…or at least show them a comical terror response.

At the same time, of course, they are profoundly *torn* because this curiosity cannot be freely exercised; it is pitted against eons of survival instinct. This is the instinct behind a minority of Sasquatch behaviors, which fall into the category of mean-spirited or intimidating, even violent; our two species have been vying for territory, for resources, and for general supremacy over untold millennia; some of that animosity spills over into today. At times, habituators do not feel welcome even in *their own yards*. You will see some of this vividly reflected in the accounts to follow, especially as connected to North Carolina (page 4), to Iowa (pages 53-55), and to Texas #2.

Sasquatch, like our own race, are distinct individuals, marked by personality differences, their traits and propensities distributed across the population in a bell curve. A few are brutal, a few are stupid, but *only* a few. People like Rick Dyer and Justin Smeja would much rather, for their own purposes, lump all Sasquatch together under a narrow, manageable definition, such as "Monster" or "mere animal." This is far easier than coping with the true breadth and complexity of the subject before us.

The material contained in this book is also contained in last year's publication, *Sasquatch Rising 2013: Dead Giants Tell No Tales: How DNA Breakthroughs and Backyard Visits Reveal the Greatest Story of Our Time*.

But since the earlier book is more than three times thicker—covering my own Vermont habituation project; subsequent visits to Texas #2 in 2010 and 2011; and recent developments in our field, such as cutting-edge genetic and linguistic research—I wanted to make available a more streamlined, affordable version that presents just the main habituation testimonials themselves. For it is these detailed accounts that can most effectively help mainstream culture to grasp the specific qualities of our zoological next of kin, to assemble a highly textured infrastructure of knowledge and compassion, and lead ultimately to the construction of a solid legal barrier between Sasquatch and its would-be trophy hunters. Yes, the first man to produce a Sasquatch body is becoming rich and famous; we can only hope that the *second* man to do so will spend the rest of his life in jail.

Christopher Noël
Northeast Kingdom, Vermont
March 1, 2014

North American Habituation Sites

As of today, I am aware of twenty-three active sites, of which I have permission to share the accounts of six, below, largely in the habituators' own words. The handful accessible to me represents merely a tiny, self-selected cross-section of habituators—those intent upon comparing notes with fellow habituators and with certain outsiders. Given this, and setting aside the vast number of similar cases that must have accrued over centuries, over *millennia*, these twenty-three can well be multiplied many-fold to estimate at least several hundred such situations now unfolding across North America. These involve both reluctant "hosts" and the fascinated folks who interact with Sasquatch within a self-contained economy of trust, and who will never risk exposing their private experiences, or their visitors, to the world at large.

Of course, all identities and locations of those contributing to this book have been kept in the strictest confidence.

Freud famously called dreams "the royal road to the unconscious," and my belief is that habituation sites are the royal road to understanding Sasquatch. Rather than taking the arbitrary and heavy-handed shots in the dark so common these days—nighttime "expeditions" and stakeouts on which we howl, whoop, and wood-knock in hopes of eliciting a response—we can gain far richer access by paying humble, receptive attention in places where the Sasquatch themselves have *chosen* to reveal facets of their nature. Indeed, an inviting posture (as opposed to an alienating one) sets the most promising stage not only for our own learning process but also for a healthy exchange of reality between our two species.

1. North Carolina

The speaker is a forty-eight-year-old woman whom we will call Ammi. Her husband "hates" what has been happening on their property for the past five years, but her son, now twenty-two, has worked with her to learn more. Beyond their yard is extremely thick forest and a vast swampland that extends seventy-two miles northeast. Occasionally, her six-year-old granddaughter visits and talks to "the hairy kids in the woods."

From 2002

It was back when we were living somewhere else, five years ago, and out here remodeling this house every day. Very first thing was a god-awful, gut-wrenching scream that came from our woods one day. My son and I both thought it sounded like a young child being raped or torn apart. There is an elementary school near here, and we believed someone was hurting a child in there. We both ran into that area of the woods, and looked, but saw nothing. I went back to the field, to make sure someone wasn't getting away, and my son continued to look around in that area of the woods. He said he never saw anyone, but it looked like someone had been there, because a lot of plants and grasses were laid down and flattened. We heard the same scream, in the same area, a few days later, but same results, on searching. There was an obvious path we hadn't noticed before, so my son checked the area off and on, at random times for about a week.

Then, from different parts of the woods over different times, we'd hear what we thought was humans trying to break into the place or coming up here. We weren't staying over here all the time, like I said. We thought there were people running through the woods. We shot at them. We've called the Sheriff's Department out here several times, too many times. Nobody ever found anything. My son chased them, never could catch up with anybody. And that went on for a long time.

What really brought it to a head was, we rented a backhoe and went to dig the ditches, and when I did that they started throwing stuff at me. Mud and sticks. I really didn't know what was going on, so I had some BFRO investigators come out. They came out three different times and did an overnight. The first time they came out they found footprints and they did some hollers and got some answers, did some wood-knocking and got some answers, and that kind of blew us all away. We were like, Oh okay, we got Bigfoots. I mean, we kind of thought the place was haunted for years. But then once we found out, my son and I just really got interested in it. We started trying to study them. Daily. We started going out there and trying to communicate with them, and basically just went from there.

I've got one group on one side of the house that's pretty receptive and friendly and we've come quite a ways. On the other side, behind the barn, they're mean. I've only been doing this about three months.

They hide really good. Even right in front of you. How would I know that? By taking pictures behind my back. I can hear them, and know they come very close, and from the sound of movement when I turn around, I suspected they may show out behind me. So the thought came to do the backwards camera trick. I pretend I am shooting in another direction, and just turn the camera backwards. Then I compare these shots to the ones I take straight on.

I also know by hearing them, all the sounds they make, but hardly ever seeing them. By watching my woods change here daily. In all these years I've only ever seen them three times.

You would just have to experience the thickness of my brush. You could hide an elephant in there. The pictures I'm taking now are winter pictures. In the summertime, those vines, you can't see from your waist down. They could crawl around under your feet and tickle your toes and you wouldn't know it.

I believe what makes them stay here is that our area is very quiet, with a good source of food and water. There's not a lot of traffic. We don't go out in the woods a lot. They've been here before we were here. It's not that they moved in, they just didn't move out.

The nice ones, when I feed them, sweet potatoes and apples and bananas, they sometimes leave me gifts. I keep them all in a small bowl. Pretty rocks. One of the rocks is studded all through with large garnets. One looks like some kind of petrified bone...maybe a hip and part of the socket, from some little animal. The rest are lots of quartz, and some is just plain rocks. I also got a civil war grapeshot cannon ball, and half of some kind of old metal bullet mold. And I got a little ceramic duck that looks like it has spent some time in the swamp.

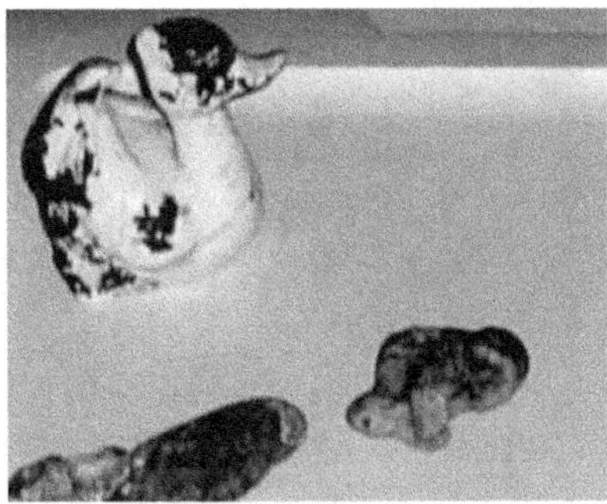

The mean ones, out behind the barn, they killed my dog and left me his skull and some bones on the work table over there. He must have been bothering them.

It was very hard to accept, but we moved on. I have had worse times. You get over stuff, and move on.

I want to let people know that there are some down sides to this too. I will study them while they stay, but if they moved on tomorrow, I would just get back to a "normal" life here. I wouldn't go looking for them anywhere else. Some days I don't want to deal with them here. But I try to keep it steady, so I can learn more.

It's a whole game of building trust with them, and it doesn't just include handing them food and walking away. People would probably think I was crazy. I go out there and I talk to the woods. I walk around, I speak to them, I sing to them, my son plays guitar for them.

My son is twenty-two. He and I are the only ones doing the study here. He occasionally brings in one friend, and it took repeated visits, but now they come close and vocalize when he is here also. He is eighteen.

I definitely know they know when I'm there. I think they know every time I step out this door because I hear them whistle. They give little whistles to I guess kind of let each other know that you're coming out. From area to area in the yard they whistle the same way. Different little whistles different places.

They imitate my son, and say, "Mom!" loudly, they can sound just like him. I thought he was playing when I was here alone, and then when he was with me talking to me.

When Rita [BFRO researcher] was visiting here, the one who tries to imitate me followed us from the house, to the swamp side, and kept whistling to us. I've been trying to teach him the tune from *Kill Bill* (when the nurse is walking down the hall). He is really trying to get that tune down, and gets quite persistent with it, if I don't do it back for him. He was back out there again today with me, and trying again. He has the first part down, and is getting pretty good at the second part. He is only about two notes off now, and he whistles the two, but not in the right tune.

(You can take a brief video tour of the property, shot by Ammi herself, and listen to the Sasquatch attempting to whistle this tune, at YouTube: "Faces in the Foliage: North Carolina Habituation Site.")

It is so amazing to hear it, because it is so different than any other sounds of the woods. At times, he just keeps repeating it over and over, like I do to teach him. They are such mimics! I always wonder if he is the same one who follows me around and does the "babbling brook" noise. Rita has heard that one.... and she can explain it to you, because she got such a kick out of it here.

From Rita, BFRO member and Ammi's research assistant; she first visited the property in December 2007

Poor thing. She was taking pictures with a 3.5 MP camera with no zoom through a pair of binoculars. That just tugged at my photographer's heartstrings. You know, if she's got Bigfoot in her backyard, she needs a decent camera.

She pays close attention to her swamp and monitors it daily for every little change. When she shares a photograph, she's already compared it to reference photos, so she knows that the figure in the shot is worth a closer look.

I saw this for myself today. Imagine seeing a large form of deep inky blackness behind some brush. So dark that it absorbs all light--like black fur would do. And then suddenly, silently, it's gone and you see browns, tans and greens where it once was. Someday, we'll get a great shot, or a shot that becomes great with the right enhancement. And it may take a long time to get that great shot. Or it may be tomorrow.

I saw more than one dark figure that disappeared after we spotted it; I heard knocking, whistling, bad dog bark mimicry, two incredibly loud and angry thumps, and other odd noises. I had one mimic my whistles. I saw tons of stick structures, trails blocked, trees snapped and in some cases huge logs that had been moved from place to place for some unknown purpose.

It's my opinion that through situations like hers, and with her determination to study these creatures in a peaceful setting, we will learn more about them than we could through other means.

A zoomed-in crop from one of Ammi's photos. The resolution is so poor because the original shows a much wider visual field, and the figure is at least 150 feet away, sitting in the swamp, nearly impossible to pick out because nearly the same color as its surroundings.

So, we sat around and chatted for a little while, and then we went outside. She feeds them fruit and sweet potatoes. She called them, and I actually heard them walk toward us. There was a group of about six or eight walking toward us and you could hear the leaves just crunch crunch crunch crunch. You couldn't see them. They started walking from a distance of I'd guess fifty yards or so, and approached probably as close as about sixty feet. But the entire time they were behind this screen of evergreen, brush, and vines. They have actually built screens in her swamp made out of these vines and trees.

You could clearly hear them approaching and that was just a fantastic experience. I mean, I was blown away, and I thought I'd be able to get a picture of them because there was a break in this screen, and I thought, Okay, when they walk across that I got 'em, I'm gonna get a picture. But oh no, they stopped just as they got to it. They were just too smart to come out in the open. And we heard some whistling, and we heard the chit-chit-chit-chit-chit of maybe rocks or Ammi was thinking walnuts, being clicked together. And they imitated the sound of a babbling brook. I found that actually kind of humorous because babbling brooks don't start and stop like you flick a light switch. And they also don't move. And during the course of the afternoon, as she was showing me around the place, the babbling brook followed us, which I just thought was funny.

So she basically threw the fruit and the sweet potatoes toward where they were. I think they just see where stuff lands, and then they come later and pick it up when she's not around or when nobody's looking, or possibly wait until dark.

We walked around a little bit and I was trying to get some pictures, and it was really interesting because you could actually see dark fur appear behind the brush, and then it would disappear. And of course she's got several photos that look like that, it's just a dark form that you can see through the brush. And it's challenging from a photographic standpoint because it's hard to photograph anything black anyway, because black is black because it absorbs all light, so if you're talking about dark animals in shadows, you're just out of luck. But that doesn't mean we don't try.

One of the more profound experiences I had that afternoon was getting "zapped," twice.

This was over on the other side of her yard, where they're not quite so friendly. It's where they had put the skull of the dog that they had killed on a work table. The table is strong. You know, it's one of those old-fashioned tables that a farmer would have put together to work on outside, really hefty. We looked at the table and thought, Okay, so this is where the skull is. And then we walked down into the woods there. All of a sudden I felt nervous, I felt a little nauseated, my head was bothering me. I felt very unwelcome. She started some similar symptoms. We stayed down there a few minutes, took a few pictures, and then we came back out.

We walked a little ways further down and ended up with some very thick brush between us and the barn so we could not see the barn. And we're poking around, trying to take pictures and stuff, and all of a sudden we hear this THUNK! up at the barn, and we're like, What was that? And then we heard it again. So we figured that we had upset someone that came up and pounded on the table.

I walked up there, with my video function on my camera running, and didn't see anything, that I *remember*, because once I got over there and I turned off my video camera I got another infrasound experience. It's like when you're about to put your hand on a TV screen, you get that tingling all over the surface of your hand, it was like that all over my whole body, and worse on my arms and legs. And I said something to her about it, and then I stepped backwards.

In my mind, it only took two seconds. But she informed me later, "Oh no, you were frozen and staring straight ahead for about twenty seconds." And…I didn't take her seriously, but I happened to have an audio recorder in my hand, so I played it back and you could tell by the beep when I turned off the video function on my camera, and when I spoke to her. I actually spoke to her twice, and then you hear when I finally do step backwards. It was a total of thirty-six seconds.

It's very interesting to me that I only remember it taking a couple of seconds. So when you hear about some people becoming disoriented and possibly losing time when they have an infrasound experience, I feel like that was an example of it. It was a very profound feeling, I've never felt anything like it. And it was a little scary too, I'll be honest, it was kind of scary. And she didn't go over to that area until a couple of minutes later, and that's when she discovered that one of the boards on the table had actually been broken and bashed in. Somebody down there just was not happy that we had walked into his woods. And we only walked in about forty feet, we didn't go far, but I think that evidently was too far.

Back to Ammi

Yesterday, when Rita and I went out, she stayed closer to the edge of the woods, and I really wasn't going to venture that far back in there but my curiosity can get a little better of me and there was some stuff I wanted to look at. I got down in the area and took me some pictures and I didn't feel too welcome. Just a little uneasiness, so I decided I'd come out, call the dogs. When I started walking back out, that's when it hit me in all the large muscles in my legs and in my rear end. My legs pretty much just buckled. I just kept going. I got real disoriented. At one point I left the little path and was walking through brambles and Rita had to holler at me and let me know which direction to back off to get back on the path. It was very visible in there. I could see her, she could see me, we could converse pretty easily. I wasn't that far from her. But my legs didn't really want to work. The best way to describe it is, I've lived in the northern states and if you've ever tried to walk through a three-foot snow drift, or running in water, that's pretty much how it felt to try to move them legs. By the time I got up to where Rita was, it started easing off a little bit, and the thing that was really weird was when we hit the edge of the woods, as soon as I stepped out of the woods into the field, it disappeared, the whole thing just disappeared.

There are so many little things they do that have nothing to do with collecting hard evidence of them, but is just fun and lets me see and hear the behaviors. That is my main focus here...I want to know all about them. Having the young ones so close here is a delight most of the time. In the same way for me as I loved watching and hearing my own kids play, and grow up. I tend to get comfortable with them being playful, and am reminded with a not so gentle zap, or growl, that I am too close, or somewhere they don't want me. Then I back up for a day, and get right back out there and try again. I am trying to come up with different ways to do things, to see what works.

When my grandchild was here last year, at age six, she used to walk near the woods and talk to herself constantly. She would take her toys and play there too. I would be gardening, and ask her who she was talking to. She would say the hairy people in the woods, or the hairy kids in the woods. I thought she had a good imagination. I didn't know anything about the Bigfoots back then.

She was walking near the “nest.” This is a long strip of land, next to the swamp, and bordered by the wood area, until it hits my yard. It is made up of loads of evergreen brush, vines, and stick add-ons. There are two and in some places three "screens,” along the side towards me. These are made of vines with added sticks, logs, brush and leaves. They have been built up even more near my house, daily. The one near the back of the pumphouse used to be easy to take pictures through, and is now almost a solid wall of debris.

I would say the nest ranges from ten to thirty feet wide, in places. It is at least fifty yards long because that structure is not all vines there, it is also laced with a lot of small sticks and branches.

Other people, habituators that I talk to who do this at their places, and do have kids, say that the Bigfoot are always watching the kids play, and they get a lot of the best pictures when they are doing that. They are the ones who told me the Bigfoot love the stuffed toys they put out, and will keep them. Other toys are moved and scattered at night, or taken, but are always returned eventually.

So I am going to try that. I will be leaving them near the feeding and nesting area, and see what happens.

I was also told they like plastic flower pots, and that explains why mine are always ending up in the woods here. I do have three boxes of old toys in the barn. And they get scattered a lot, and stacked on each other. I hadn't thought of it being them. I just blamed the dogs.

January 23rd, 2008

Tonight, they have been playing games on my roof, since it got dark. The porch roof is right by a tree, and then they climb onto the house roof. They've tossed rocks and a branch down my chimney, in the last few minutes. I went out into the cold twice, but of course they are gone, or ducking over the roofline.

My dogs have been going nuts, and judging from the new branches in my walkway they must be throwing at them too.

Last time they did this, they tossed pieces of bricks down the bedroom chimney and woke hubby up, then a handful of live lizards came down...freaked him out...he hates lizards...made me catch them all.

This has made me think of something, though. They do seem to be very active in the colder weather. Thinking back on my days before I knew it wasn't humans trying to mess with me here, it happened more in the colder days than in the summer.

So far, it has been smaller ones up there. I think the juveniles play those games. I hope none of the big guys ever take a notion to go up...could damage my dome.

I have floodlights on the house, and turn them on when they climb up there, or pound on the house. I turn them off after a couple hours, and it has stopped them before, did tonight also.

I do tolerate the tapping on windows and at the electric box.

That is done more gently, and for attention, so I treat it as such, and just tap back from in here, or talk to them loud enough for them to hear me. It is a game that is played for a while, then I usually have to be the one to stop it.

My husband refuses to believe, as in, everything can be explained by deer or owls. Yep, we had a fun debate about who dropped the bricks and lizards down the chimney. He has heard them, and refuses to go behind the barn at all. He used to say there was nothing out there, but now he slips up, and he talks about them some. He just hates the whole thing, and would rather I do what his mom's family did when they were living here in the past, and just ignore and deny them. He really only gets mad when his mom starts in on him about me studying them. But she doesn't say they are not here, just that I shouldn't "mess around with things I don't know about."

When Rita came and brought the camera here, as soon as she left, he started to move the couch from in front of the window that faces the swamp. I asked him what he was doing, and he said, "I thought you could get the best shots from here."

I said, "Shots of what?"

He got mad and said, "I was just trying to help!!"

I just laughed, and helped him move the couch.

February 4th, 2008

I had an interesting day here. I had a half-frozen lizard on my kitchen steps, rare, because they usually are under something in this weather. It was thirty-five degrees out today. And this little guy was so cold he couldn't move, thought he was dead at first. Hubby had just come in that same door, not long before I went out and found the lizard. Maybe it was meant as a little gift for him?

I saw in front of the door the bag I'd left chips and Cheetos out in, near the woods, so I went to check the pumphouse, where it had been hanging, about six feet up inside. Gone from there. I went around the pumphouse to look, and found some small footprints, about the size of our six- or seven-year-old grandkids'. One was almost perfect, so I got pictures. Still don't have casting materials here.

Went and picked up the bag, and took it, and popped the lizard inside, so I wouldn't be shunning a "gift." (I later snuck him back out and tucked him under a pile of leaves.)

I put the bag on the big table, behind the barn. While I had my back to the woods, the dogs went nuts towards the woods, so I turned to see one of them chasing after something that I couldn't see, into the nest area. The pups were looking at something hard, just under where the stuffed teddy bear is hanging, so I went to check that out. The ground had been dug up and dirt was all over on top of the leaf litter, so I went in closer. Ewwwww! A fresh deer leg, no skin, half of a pelvis, the thigh, knee, and part of the leg. Still all connected, and half full of meat, the other half chewed off. The hoof had been broken off. The whole thing was still warm, even though it was freezing out.

This was only about five or six feet from where I had picked up the bag, so I couldn't believe I hadn't seen it then. (Later checked the pic I took of the bag, and nope, it wasn't there then.) I don't want to turn down "gifts"...and know they have "gifted" other habituators with deer, so I made a big deal over it, and giving it to my dogs, who wouldn't touch it at first, but then one finally grabbed it and ran off with it.

I thanked the wookies out loud, and headed inside.

I want to study behavior, share what I am doing so others can have some idea what it is like to do this, and mainly have me and the critters here, left to live in peace. I do bring some people in, for the study, who have the skills needed to try to get some evidence, but it is done quietly, and not in crowds. The BF react to different ones, different ways. I note that, and try to figure out that also.

They are most active if I am alone and tend to hang back more if even my hubby is out there. They do favor my son being out with them, at times, but he has a pretty strange way of playing with them, and will go out alone to do that at night.

I get more good reaction with the younger ones, and the mammas and day ones. The night ones scare me at times. My son gets reactions at night, good and bad, but he is twenty-two and "bullet-proof," so he takes more risks than I do, and enjoys doing so, or can at least run back inside quicker. I can, however, sit quietly for hours, and just listen, and look for them. I can go out and sit close to the area, and sing, hum, whistle, play "Peek-a boo," use myself as entertainment, like you would for a toddler, and make a total fool of myself, just to try to get a reaction from them. And then sit there even longer, ignoring them, to try to make them get me to react, which gets me movement, and vocals, and maybe a picture. That is what I do the most, and it seems to be working, as far as getting them used to me, and accepting me being there some. I push it too much at times, and then have to back off a few days. It goes on like that.

I have learned that if I ignore them totally, don't raise my blinds, and don't go outside at all, by around noon or one pm, they will come up and tap on a window near me...easy....or jiggle the tag on the electric box, next to where I sit here, on the computer. I always have rewarded that, by pulling up the blinds, and taking them out a treat. They know that now, so it is a regular thing, if I do that. No, I am not going to jump up and run snapping a camera, it would totally mess up what little trust they have, which is more important than a "great picture right now." If I can build the trust more, I will have much greater chances for a very good close-up shot. I have that kind of patience.

March 17th, 2008

Today, I spoke to my neighbor on the other side of my swamp. He had called me over there to take some pics of his pups...he has no computer or camera. He wants to have me help find them homes. I went over and took the pics, and was getting ready to go, and he asked me if I had ever heard or seen anything "strange" in the swamp, since I had been here. I told him, "Yes, plenty," and he went on to describe all the sounds. He has had two sightings, believes they are "a people, and not devils," and described being paced, and zapped. He asked me if I ever heard one whistle a "funny little tune," and when I whistled the *Kill Bill* song, he said, "THAT'S IT!!!"

I told him I had taught it to them, and he now wants to see if we can teach them "Amazing Grace," if we work from both sides on it. So I'm game for that one!

May 14th, 2008

We got some bad tornadoes through this area a few days back—eleven in this part of the state alone that night. We were in bed, and just before a storm hit here, someone outside our window said very loud, "Wah-Coh'-Too!" Just that one word, but it woke up my husband. I hadn't fallen asleep yet, and heard it clearly. It was like it was yelled at the window. It then sounded like someone tried to lift the back window. Frank jumped up, and headed toward the window, and about then, the storm winds hit hard. We both dove into a closet, until it passed. It didn't touch down right here, but just down the road.

It got really scary for a while, but all we lost was some large limbs here. Frank was getting mad, because I was excited that I finally heard one of their words clearly. I was saying, "Do you think it means, 'Wake up!' or that it is their word for 'tornado'?"

He says, "Who gives a shit, I'm in a friggin' storm, and you are worried about them?"

I said, "Yep, they worried about us, and they are still outside."

That just pissed his puppet more, so I shut up about it.

I still wonder what that word means.

May 18th, 2008

Had a bit more fun today....a poor soul broke down on the road in front of my house, with a cycle. I have to admit, I took some zoom shots first, from the porch, before I saw how scared he was getting. He actually got off the bike, and tried to hide behind it. Said my dogs were creeping him out, barking at him. He said the barks were coming from the dogs, and echoing behind him...poor guy was really scared. Never saw anyone load a bike so quick.

I didn't explain the wooks or the infrasound to him...just let him think it was the dogs. Actually, one dog was barking, but the rest were just laying there watching him. The one kept barking when I came out. He commented how she seemed to "look right thru him." She was barking at the wooks behind him.

They backed up out of the wheat when I came out to the road, and I fussed at them about scaring him, when he left. I'm sure they got a kick out of it. I got a "fear wave" of infrasound when I fussed at them, and told them, "Nice try, it don't work on me anymore, I know what it is." It stopped.

It is going to be a strange summer, knowing about them this year.

I searched some online for Indian words. The closest I could find is Apache. “ya-kos'” = “clouds,” and “tu'” = “water.” Together it would sound very close to what I heard.

May 22nd, 2008

I found two ripe mulberries on my art easel today....Wow...I went straight to the tree, didn't know they had dropped. The ground was clean under the tree, except for one small pile left there. Guess I'm on rations for those.

Can't blame them, I love them too. That explains why they have left my strawberries alone for a few days. Well, at least they are sharing this year. They didn't do anything else at the easel yet....just swiping a bottle of paint every couple days, and leaving me "gifts".... mostly rocks, and a few pinecones.

Even now, I still feel some days that I am no closer to knowing them than when I started. And really I'm not. Nights can still get crazy on a whim, but those have gotten to be more rare than normal here now. There are a few of them who interact, and respond to me here, when they want to, but it is never on demand, anytime I want. They still won't just come out and show themselves, without it being accidental, or as a threat, a brief move. And I still piss them off when I cut the grass, or go into my woods for any reason. They let me know, by disrespecting my house, and hitting on it, climbing up on the roof or porch just to make noise, or irritating the dogs to keep them barking all night.

I can also draw a whizzed-by pinecone, stick, or dirt clod, if I am mowing. So I let hubby mow now. I have pics of him yelling at the woods here, and just staring them down. He has given up on the total unbelief in them existing, and has settled into just not wanting to discuss them at all.

I think I have established that the house is ours. But they still claim the outside, including the outbuildings here. And we have a day/night sharing of the yard. But they want it left alone.

The garden I planted is mine, but they feel free to "trade me" my crops for rocks, sticks, pinecones, feathers, and bits of trash they find, of any kind. Occasionally, I get a dead bird, turtle, frog, or rodent. "Mmmm...wookie stew" is all I can say when I find it raided, and those in the place of it. "Wookie stew" is a running joke between me and my hubby, when he asks on the phone from work, "What's for dinner tonight?" Hubby really hates that joke. They still consider all of the old fruit trees and berries here as theirs, and have let me know that.

They do make me smile and laugh at times. Sometimes one will abandon the usual bird and animal calls, for a funky sound, to get my attention. Taking all of my garden tools and stacking them all up together. Lining pinecones in a circle, around my flower beds. I find pinecones in the strangest places here.... and that always makes me smile. I guess I like that they care to make me smile and laugh. It makes me feel as if I am gaining some trust with them. Sometimes I wonder if there are just one or two that "get a kick" out of watching the old woman happy, while the rest just still hate me being here at all. One of those things I want to know, but may be better off not knowing.

I have learned to be vocal here with them. I tell them if I like something they have done, and if I don't. It's the mom in me...I have to "train everyone" to get along together, like I did when my kids where young. Or like a new relationship and the "control games" to establish the boundaries. Only now, it's me and some people I can't usually see, sometimes can't hear, and whose language I don't know. I think they do understand English. I just don't know the other language they speak. I think it is a very old native language, and like ours, has probably
developed its own slang thru time.

Sometimes I enjoy them being here, and other times I wish my life was normal, and I didn't know about them. Normal as in, not discussing or arguing about what the people in our woods are doing, or have done. Normal as in Frank not yelling at me, “STOP INTERACTING WITH THEM!”

There are days when I try to interact with them, and days when I just ignore them. They do the same with me...days of interaction, and days you wonder where they are, as they are so quiet. I worry about them in stormy, very cold, and very hot weather.

I wonder how they deal with the bugs, as the biting flies and mosquitoes get bad here. Then I remind myself that they have never done it different, and are probably fine.

The hardest thing is pretending not to hear or notice them, when people who don't know stop in, and they decide to give a mid-day owl/dog chatter/bark and whistle number, from the nearby brush. When it stops your guests in their tracks, and they are staring at the spot it came from, and looking at you, or asking questions you don't want to answer, well it can be funny to me at times. I have a bad habit of laughing at that, and offering no explanation except "Yeah, that was weird." I have lost a few friends over that. But I would rather they think it is this place that is haunted, or strange, than tell them, and them think me crazy. I have done both, so I opt for the "strange place" and just meet them elsewhere, for company.

Finding out that my closest neighbor also knows about them helped a lot. It was a very awkward conversation start for us both, to learn it. "What do you hear?" "Have you ever heard...seen…?" Once we both realized we both knew, it was great. Plus we are both relieved that we have the places on both sides of their sleeping area, so we know they won't be bothered there. We agree that our nights are better spent in our houses. Seems they also have that night ownership in his yard too. It took us five years to have that conversation. Mainly, because he thought my dogs were stealing his chickens. Once I was able to tell him they have been known to "trade" for chickens too, we have gotten along better, though he wasn't aware of the "gift/trade value" of the local pinecones and rocks! He had never actually seen one of my dogs over there, but he had found some strange stuff in his chicken house. It also explained how the "dogs" were getting the coop unlatched. I had lost rabbits from cages here the same way.

May 28th, 2008

I did my easel thing here. Set it up right at the very edge of the woods, and with my back to them. I painted a pic of one peeking thru leaves, and left it and blank paper out. The first night they swiped (er traded for) a bottle of bright metallic blue, for two dead baby snapping turtles, and left paint splattered all over my chair, the ground, and the surrounding leaves.

When I found it the next day, I painted a picture of one of the turtles, and left it there, with some blank paper on the side. That night, they "painted" all over my easel, my pic, the paper next to it, the chair, leaves. Looked like a three-year-old got ahold of it. They gained a bottle of pink, and a sky blue that night. They also scattered my brushes all over the ground, around and under my chair.

The ground around the easel looked like I had eighty people stomping around it for a week, completely mashed and compacted down hard. A new very stomped trail appeared from the woods, leading directly to that spot.

Rain had me bring it up on the porch, where it has been since. I have heard them play around there late at night, and find a bottle or brush moved now and then, but no more painting, nor have they taken anything. They have left a few gifts, like a ripe mulberry on my easel. My kids are grown, so now I have some new "art" to hang on my fridge!

May 31st, 2008

I went out to water the garden today, and took my camera. I was home alone, and when I got to one side of the house, I decided to "make a rainbow" with the spray, into the sunlight there, partly to amuse myself.

So I was spraying away, and snapping pics, and I started thinking about when my granddaughter stayed with me last year, and how she loved to see me make rainbows, and she would play in the spray, running in and out, and singing "Somewhere Over the Rainbow" with me. I started singing it out loud, and was doing a silly little dance we used to do together, and didn't notice or hear hubby pull in the driveway from work. He walked up behind me, to see what I was doing, and here I was, just spraying the hose in the air, and singing, and dancing away.

He laughed really loud, and it made me jump and stop. He said something about how I had finally just lost it, and started back to get his stuff from the car.

After dinner, I sat down to check the pics. Wow, seems our friends liked the rainbows too!

And the hose. I have woken up many mornings to find the hose on, and have the water bills to prove it. Hubby always blames me for forgetting and leaving it on. Like even when it was spraying all over the porch, towards the front door...like I just walked thru the spray, inside, and didn't notice it was on?

The last time, I fussed and yelled at them about not turning it off, and it has been on two times since, but the nozzle has been shut to close the spray.

They also empty my dog tub at night. It holds fifteen gallons, and they will empty it, on hot days, when I have just refreshed it. This winter, I got pics of a five-gallon bucket that went missing here, and showed up in the woods near the pump house, sitting upright, full to the brim with fresh water. I think I busted them trying to carry it off, and they just sat it down and hid. It was on the start of one of the trails that leads to the nest area. I left it there, and it disappeared that night, and the empty bucket showed back up in the pumphouse the next night. So I have set up another tub, near that woods area, and kept it with fresh water. Nope, they never touched it, but they still hit the dog's tub. I figured they trust more what they know I leave for my dogs.

I see them dart across that area at lot, out of the corner of my eye. I think that is what Frank is seeing too. He will turn suddenly, and just stare. That or he got popped with another pine cone, or a stick, for ending the rainbow dance. He usually gets mean when they pop him.

He did go out and take the trimmers to the yard edges, and he really cut up some of the areas they like to hide and watch in. I was kinda mad he did that, but I know they mess with him from those areas, when he mows, so I just figured he is trying to keep them back off him some.

He got ill with me just now when I asked him why such a severe trim job there. Has to be hell at times, being him.

June 5th, 2008

Hubby came walking with me around, just going on dusk. He was picking with me, because I found a pile of sticks, next to the back of the barn, and I took pics, and took one piece that looked chipped up, and put it in my pocket.

I was pretty surprised he stayed with me, as I went behind the barn looking...where he usually won't go. Well it didn't last long, next thing I knew, I heard him make a kind of "hmmmptf" sound, and he turned and was walking fast towards the house.

I had just heard some twigs snapping, and rustling, close, and figured it spooked him. Oh well. I turned back around to look where I had heard it and…they just sat there, and let me take two pics. Then I felt strange just taking pics, and I lowered the camera. They turned and left. I stood there a minute, and then went into the house to see if hubby had seen them.

He was sitting on the couch, looking at the TV, and wouldn't even look at me, but he was shook up. I started to ask him if he saw them and he just yelled, "OK...I DON'T WANT TO TALK ABOUT IT!! EVER!" And then he went and got in bed. I went in the bedroom, and he shoved my pillows at me, and said, "Just leave me alone tonight, please."

So I am on the couch tonight I guess.

I guess he saw them...

They were like in a pile. Little furry ones, kind of stacked in a pyramid shape.

Well, that was a definite first here. I'm still trying to process it, and am wondering why they did that, and if they will do it again. I can't even joke about this one. Not feeling scared, just don't really know what to think about it.

I haven't heard them at all tonight, and the dogs are not up and barking like they usually do. Come to think of it, the dogs usually follow us all over the yard, but today, none of them came behind the barn with us. They followed us up until I found those sticks, and I didn't notice them leave, but none were around when I turned to go back to the house. They were all up on the porch.

Do you think I should leave them a gift there in the morning?

Or should I just ignore it?

I think it did kind of scare me. Not then, but now it kind of does...not knowing why they did that.

A Phone Conversation between Ammi and Myself

—I was talking to [another member of the habituators' forum] and you know what I realized?

—What?

—The other day Frank had gone and trimmed up those bushes just there, where the little ones showed out yesterday evening, severely clipped those things. I was really torqued with him that he did that. And he got ill with me, talking about, "Oh, you just trying to give them things a place to—" And I said, "Yeah, because that's the way they are, y'know, you gotta give 'em respect." And I said, "That's why you're getting napped with pinecones." And then he says, "I don't believe in that crap!" And I'm like, "Yeah okay, it's the dogs and the deers and the owls throwing that shit…"

So when I went outside, I apologized to them. I was talking to the woods, y'know, and I was telling them, "You know I would never—'cause I'm the one that usually does the trimming—I would never, ever trim this so severe." And I said, "He's just an idiot. He refuses to believe in you. I know you guys are throwing stuff at him." I said, "I wish you would just step out in front of him."

—Oh, and this was just a few days before the episode?

—Two days before.

—When I was talking to [fellow habituator], I was saying, "Why did they do that?"

And I said, "Well you know he trimmed up that hedge over there, that bush." And as I said that I said, "Oh my God!" Have you ever got that feeling, like when someone hits a certain note in a song, where you get that tingle all the way through your body? Well, that's what it was like, I knew that was it. I got that tingle from my head to my toes.

—So they were in the same place that would've been hidden if he had not trimmed the bushes back in there?

—Yes sir. They sure were. They were crouched down like they were hiding behind the same bush but it wasn't there. And they were in a pyramid, a pile of them.

—What size were they?

—Different. Different sizes.

—Were there two?

—Two? No, there was a pyramid of them. I felt stupid. I still felt stupid this morning, because here all this time I've been feeding these things, trying to interact with them, thinking what you want is an interaction with them, y'know. And what did I do when they finally showed themselves? I took pictures of them like they were some kind of freak show. I didn't say a word to them. I just took two pictures and then stood there realizing how stupid it was, so I just lowered the camera and stood there staring at them. Still didn't know what to say. And when they left, they didn't stand up and turn around or nothing. They just faded backward into shadow, and the foliage. It was pretty deep dusk. You can't make out details in the pictures, just general shapes. It was maybe a minute or less between when I put the camera down and they faded.

—But before that, you got the chance to really feast your eyes on these folks.

—Yeah, and they looked just as confusing as…I figured out why so many of the pictures are so confusing. I'm going to be able to pick them out better from now on. They stack up on each other. You got arms and legs and faces all tangled together from a whole bunch of them. That's why it's looking so weird.

—And like the little ones are gripping onto the fur and…

—I mean, some of them are laying down, some got their heads stuck in sideways. Some are over from the top. They got their arms over top of their head.

—Ah, just to mess with your eyes?

—Yeah, it's all an eye-screw. And I was like, that's why you can't make out a clear face. One will have his hand cupped over his face, or one of them next to them's got their hand cupped over the other one's face. It's wild, and smart.

June 13th, 2008

I have always left the blinds open parts of the day, and some of the night, before bed, so they can look in here also. That is probably why if I get up and move around in here for over an hour, and don't raise those blinds, they will start to "tap tap tap" lightly on the windows. They know my reaction is to simply raise the blinds, and go about my business. They know I won't run or jump to try to see them. I may ease a camera around the corner but my face won't be with it. They are getting me trained pretty well here. They almost have me tamed, habituated.

I also know, if I don't walk around for a few days, and just ignore them, take no pics, etc., they come in closer, and get more vocal, to try to get my attention. They are like children like that. I haven't had them show out again, but I notice in the pics, they are right at the edge.

June 28th, 2008

Frank was loaded up to take his daughter back to Georgia. She and her boyfriend have been here a week, and besides one tour around our place, have stayed at his mom's house. Frank was in the car, and the boyfriend also....Robyn decided she wanted some apples from my tree, about the same time I came out to say my good-byes.

Boyfriend got out to hug me bye, Robyn was walking back from the apple tree next to the barn, and we all heard a very loud, "Frank!" yelled from behind the barn.

I had to just laugh, it was a very good imitation of my voice.

Robyn ran to the car, Frank jumped out glaring at the barn area, Boyfriend and Robyn looked at me confused.

I just kept laughing, and told Frank, “You explain it on the ride.” I looked at Robyn and Boyfriend and told them, “They are harmless, and your dad still doesn't believe in them. Ya'll have a nice safe trip home."

And I went inside...

[Author's Note: Independent photographer Jon D. Patton visited Ammi and set up his high-resolution camera on her front porch, aimed and focused just inside the thick screen of leaves at the edge of her yard. From inside the house, he then remotely snapped a shot every ninety seconds for two hours. Patton shared the resulting images with me, which I was able to render into a time-lapse animation sequence; near the end, a face and fingers briefly come to view. See this animation, another striking picture taken by Ammi herself inside a suspected "nest" area, and a brief tour of her property, on YouTube: "Faces in the Foliage: North Carolina Habituation Site."]

2. Oklahoma

The speaker is a Native American woman in her late forties. She is a medically retired police detective with a bad back that has required several surgeries. Her daughter and grandchildren are frequent visitors.

1954

One of my very first memories of a Shadow Person was on a foggy morning. The time of year was early summer. I was about four years old. My brothers and I spent hours in the woods near Ma's house. In those days families didn't worry about kids being taken. Hours were spent outdoors.

I recall Ma was cooking breakfast, as I slid out the front door headed for the woods. The woods were thick with locust trees, grasses, and moss. This particular morning the fog was thick. I wanted to see what it looked like in the woods. As I walked up the road to the entrance, I saw them, all four of them, four tall shadowy figures. They looked like an Indian family. The difference was they were all gray. The father and mother were standing behind two children. Their faces looked Indian to me, like Ma's. They were the tallest people I had ever seen. I stopped a few feet in front of them and looked at them. Their expressions didn't change as they looked back at me. To this day I still remember it felt like a dream staring at them. They had grayish hair from head to toe. There was no hair on their faces, hands and the bottoms of their feet. The hair on their bodies was probably two inches pretty much uniform in length. It lay flat against their bodies. The hair on their heads was more ruffled. As if it needed to be combed. They stood for probably only seconds. The largest one, the father I assume, turned to his right and walked away with the others following. They never made a noise. Everything was muted. They disappeared into the fog and the woods.

I walked up to where they had been standing. I remember wondering why the edge of the bank there was crumbling. I was never afraid while standing there looking at them. I was more curious than anything else. I felt lost.

Then, I turned and ran all the way back to Ma. When I entered the house I was confused. I remember telling Ma about them. She told me those were the Shadow People, leave them be. She was very adamant never to follow the Shadow People. There was a possibility if you did you would never return. Ma said that children that did follow them often get lost and confused.

For several years we ran and played in the woods always under the watchful eye of Ma. She never allowed us out to play until she checked for signs. She always checked the scents on the wind and the tracks in the sandy road. Once in a while she would not allow us out to play until late morning. She never told us exactly why, just wouldn't.

Over the next few years Ma would occasionally mention the Shadow People. After I, her persistent grandchild, insisted on it, she explained they were ancient people. They didn't bother anyone nor did they want to be bothered. There were several tribes of them. They were all people, just different than us. Ma explained they avoided people like us.

One summer day, Ma called me to her and read me an article from Readers Digest. This article was about some men that had filmed a Bigfoot [the Patterson/Gimlin Film]. Ma showed me the tiny pictures in the article and told me that was a Shadow Person. “Never bother them, it’s bad to hurt one,” she told me. “Leave them be.” They wouldn't hurt me, I should just leave them alone.

When asked to share with others the knowledge I have obtained over the years, I realize it's not as easy as it once appeared. It's complicated to talk about the Shadow People. Through the years they have been labeled with every imaginable tag—mythical, imaginary, monsters, monkeys, apes, hominids and of course unknown primates. There have been many who have chased them, begged and pleaded with them to appear.

I do not care if you question my credibility. I do not have to prove who I am or what I am. I have simply agreed to share old and new things. I cannot prove to anyone what I am sharing. You will either believe or not believe. Whatever you decide will be up to you. All photos and video were taken by myself or my family.

I only care that the Shadow People remain in peace to rear their children and live their lives. At this moment it appears many wish to murder one or a family for science. Killing one is murder. These are the ancient people of the world. Call them what you will, they have survived much and adapted to remain in the quiet areas of our world.

As I grew, every few years my path crossed with the Shadow People. Each time it was a different place, several years apart. Each one appeared different in color, shape and size. Each one was in an area I would characterize as the fringes of civilization. Never have I been threatened or harmed. Each time the Shadow Person was the one who disappeared into the shadows.

Years back, after relocating my family to a rural area, I discovered that those Shadow People were again close at hand. They are as interested in us as we are in them. They will if the opportunity arises peek in your window. They will stand back and watch you. They have never approached any member of my family or myself. I do talk to them. I always respect the personal space that we each need to maintain our relationship.

On many occasions one of the kids will be outside and come running in asking, "Did you call me?" I have been working in the gardens or sitting outside and have heard a child's voice call,

"Mom." It sounds just like one of my kids. This has happened many times over the years when I was home alone. They are known to knock on houses both day and night. Why they do this is anyone's guess. I suspect it's a form of communication, checking for a reaction.

I will never be able to answer for myself or for others all the questions about these wonderful, gentle creatures.

Summer 2007

My nine-month-old grandson Squirt was sitting in the sandbox at the time of "the monkey-chase," as the kids called it. He was reaching and laughing at the bushes where they burst out. It was his behavior that got my attention at first. He was cooing and laughing as he reached out in that direction. I thought wow he must see one of the cats.

A split second later the first one burst out of the brush and ran bouncing across the yard. I am convinced Squirt had spent several minutes watching the monkey-kids in the edge of the brush. We call them that because they look like the drawings from the rise of man or the hobbits.

Actually I knew they were coming around for years. I just kept it to myself until about five years ago and told my husband and dad. I finally had good prints to show them.

It was when I realized that so many want to kill them that I stepped forward and met others who were looking for them. I believe them to be hominin and not apes. Sorry, that's the way I was raised. I have gradually begun sharing things I have seen and heard with others. It's hard to learn to trust anyone. I decided it was time to teach the kids and grandkids the old ways also. As I was taught.

This summer just brought it all home. My little five-year-old grandson is the one, besides the nine-month-old, who can spot them hiding in the brush when no one else can. Taking pictures of the areas he says they are in generally shows shadows shaped like humans. I don't want the kids to fear these guys, I want them to learn to respect them.

But back to the monkey-chase. Just before dark, I saw three of them. The grandkids say there were five altogether, plus the babysitter. She was about the color of this little guy in the picture I took, maybe a bit more auburn.

I saw one very dark one, mouse-colored, and one red. The grandsons said there was actually three very dark ones and the two lighter ones. They were everywhere in a matter of seconds It was one of the most amazing things I have ever had happen. They burst out of the bushes, ran all around us, and the kids gave chase like a game of hide-n-seek. They won hands down. Then they were gone. They were between two-and-a-half and three-and-a-half feet tall, rail thin and fast as the wind. Along with a female about five-and-a-half feet tall hiding in the shadows and holding a baby. The babysitter kept reaching out from the brush as they would run by. She ran up and down in the brush. The most amazing thing is they never made a sound. None of them. As soon as it was over my grandchildren put out a pizza and P&J sandwiches. Which disappeared right after dark.

Here's how I got a picture, on a different night. I usually just point the camera in the direction I hear noise, and if I can tell which way it's moving, I'll point it just ahead, where I think it's going to be. This night, we were sitting outside and then I heard some rustling and I started walking around the yard. It was well after dark. My daughter and I made a big circle around the yard just snapping pictures, and when we got over by the bench, we couldn't see him, we could just hear him moving around. I ended up with forty or fifty pictures and they were just dark. A friend of mine, another habituator, has a program where she can lighten them up, and she called me and said, "Guess what you got! You got a three-foot teddy bear walking around." I couldn't believe it. Then she asked me, "Does it look like he's holding something?" I'm thinking it's one of the teddy bears, they're about ten inches long.

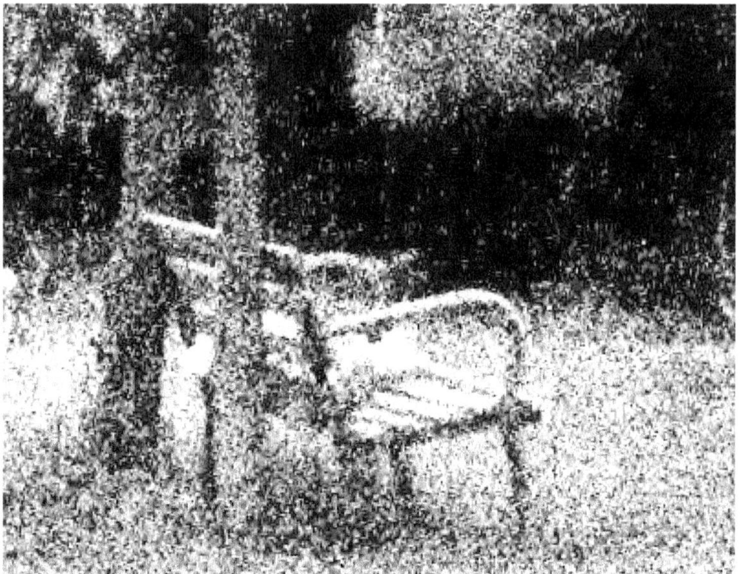

Juvenile Sasquatch photographed in nearly pitch dark, August 2007. The right hand holds a "borrowed" teddy bear; the left arm is in front of the dark body and thus not visible (don't be fooled by the bench frame)

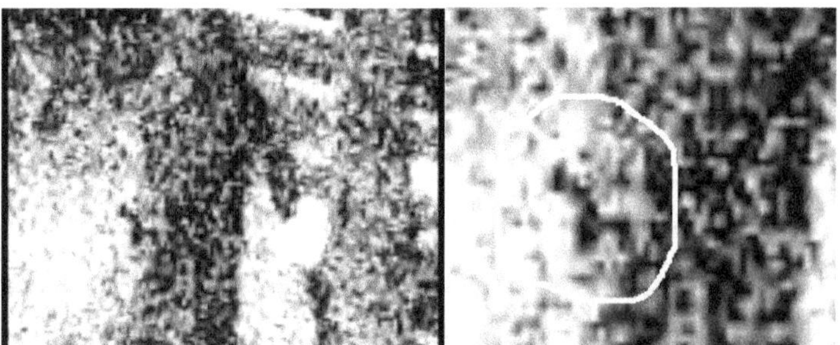

I have lived here sixteen years and they have always traveled through back and forth a couple times a week. Year-round. This year the lake came up and they hung around a lot more than in years past. However, this year the grandkids converged as a group more than usual. Generally, the kids are here one or two at a time. Plus the baby was here a lot.

I have always fed the wild animals. It's a hobby as much as compassion for the creatures the Creator has given us. This is a way of giving back to the Creator. We have so much and the little fur balls have so little. The more you feed the more they will come.

Years back we built a small garden pond, more of a frog sanctuary than anything. Stocked it with minnows and goldfish, which were promptly eaten. This was an ongoing pattern. Stock the pond and see how quickly the fish disappeared. A garden pond can be a great source of entertainment, also much work, depending on how you wish to handle it. Building an ecosystem takes time.

As each spring came and went more was added to the pond. It was during this time that the prints began to appear around it. The first bare prints measured fourteen inches by five-and-a-half inches. They appeared on the garden path beside the pond during the winter. They also appeared *in* the pond. As the footprints appeared the fish disappeared.

Each year the fruit would ripen. Just as it was ready to pick it would disappear overnight, never in the daytime. The bare footprints were different sizes. They ranged from a mere four inches long to nineteen inches long. The amazing thing about footprints: Often they are beside the paths, in the grass, as if to avoid detection.

Since the beginning of the year I have started to organize and keep a brief record of the Shadow People in my world. After the ice storm last winter we emptied two freezers of food. No idea how many pounds were placed by the habitat area. All disappeared overnight. During this time the bird feeders would often empty overnight, also, as would most of the feed on the ground.

About a month later, during the night, someone jerked on the back door. Several times, this actually broke the bottom hinge off and sprung the door. My thoughts were that the Shadow People were hungry and knew that there could be food in the freezer. Over the years we have actually lost food from the icebox and freezer, never giving much thought to it.

As the ground began to thaw there were faint tracks appearing. They once again were different shapes and sizes. We purchased a trail camera to use and play with. It isn't for serious hunting, it's merely for the enjoyment of catching our nighttime visitors. I was hooked on trying to see more.

As the winter began turning to spring, I was recording audios and some videos, never catching a Shadow Person on film. Although I believe they did walk by chattering as in a conversation. This audio was shared with several others, including researchers, for evaluation. I have hope that someday there will be an answer to what sounded like a foreign language being spoken in my yard at two AM. I have had cameras moved, picked up, set down, and turned over. I have had only shadows to show for hours of video.

We have some neighbors. I don't know most of them. They moved out here from the city and tried to make country like the city. I don't think country agrees with them that well. They are putting up cameras, lights and fences. For whatever reason!

I suspect the neighbor right next door has seen them. He is an older guy and carries a big pistol on his hip and a rifle slung on his back to walk around his yard. There for a while he creeped around in a ghillie suit. Built a brush blind and just crawled around the yard. He had an alarm that was hooked up to an air raid type siren. Imagine what fun that dang thing was. Every few minutes it was like WWII around here. Some of the other neighbors finally called the law on him.

This year, I began putting out snack food for the Shadow People. I tell them when I am putting it out that it is for them. They often are hiding in the woods nearby and I am certain they can hear me as I talk to them. This food is not in the same areas as the critters' food. I separate the food out of respect. I would not serve a guest food from the dog dish nor will I share snacks for the children of the Shadow People with the raccoons on the ground. My quirk. I was taught to respect them. At first they didn't touch the snacks. In fact, nothing touched the foods. Which was very odd. This continued for several weeks.

Then one night the snacks were taken. An audio recording of this indicated that during the rain the container the snack was in was lifted out of the tree and returned. This container was approximately eight feet from the ground.

Thus began the game of "snatch the snacks." Certain nights the snacks would be taken. Soon, I began attempting ways of catching the Folks on video. Never have I gotten more than a shadow moving or sounds that I have come to associate with the Shadow Family. On occasion I will have one container moved to another tree. Sometimes it will be higher or lower in the tree. Sometimes, I will need a ladder to take the container down to refill it.

I also leave gifts of beads, toys, balls, and other interesting objects. Sometimes, toys and balls will disappear for a period only to reappear months later. Sometimes the reappearance will last for only a day or two and then the objects will disappear again. The working assumption is that it's the Shadow Folks moving the items. At this point I have doubts that possums and coons want trinkets.

The toy house is a playhouse filled with abandoned toys not played with any longer. As the main house overflows with toys they are crated up and moved to the toy house. Only to be forgotten. This year I checked the toy house and found that most of the toys were no longer there. On occasion, I find small toys scattered over our acreage. Based on the behaviors I am observing, the Shadow People never take anything they know belongs to some member of the family. It appears they only take what is ignored. This not only includes toys. At times garden tools will disappear and reappear months later in an odd place.

We leave stuffed toys on the bench in the backyard. Sometimes by morning they are scattered all over the lawn, but sometimes they are only slightly rearranged. Or just one will be turned over, like a trick or a game, seeing if we'll notice. One morning, we found that the toy dragon was flipped.

While playing with my grandchildren one evening, I noticed a change in the birds singing. There was a snapping of tree limbs and soft noises in the brush. I started snapping pictures within the area. There is no panic feeling. No fear. We continue about our business.

I firmly believe that no harm will come to anyone who has a relationship with them. I will say never leave small children alone. Not because they will be harmed. Children can and will try to follow these guys. A small child in the bush is never a good thing.

It is truly a blessing to have even a glimpse of these wondrous people. Now, that being said, there are many reports of these creatures being frightening and dangerous. Yes that is probable and possible. I am always puzzled by these reports. What makes a creature, any creature, become aggressive? What makes a killer a killer? I will not dispute anyone's claim of aggression by a Bigfoot. I refuse to argue this point with anyone. I suspect that if there is aggression there is a reason for these actions. My thoughts are perhaps that aggression is due to getting too close to the young. Most animals, including humans, will protect their young by whatever means are at hand.

I have never witnessed aggressive behavior from the family unit that often visits us in the night. My family and I spend time out there at all hours of the day and night. Never while we are outside do we feel threatened. Watched, yes. I don't know how to describe it other than just that. Somewhere close by someone is watching.

It does, however, seem that the children and women more often have that feeling. There are possibly several reasons for this. One, the creatures watching are more interested in or entertained by children and women. Or possibly they withdraw further back when it's males about. I personally think that it's because men have a different air about them and are often the ones in the woods with guns.

Often the feeling of being watched is accompanied by soft sounds of movement. Sometimes sticks breaking or being pushed aside. It's at these times I try taking pictures of the area the noise is coming from. I have tried to school myself not to put a camera up to my eye or make a quick movement. Looking at photos taken at such times, I feel it is safe to say that most often what you will see in a photo is partial facial features. The eyes are what I notice most often. After finding an eye then I look for the other features.

I am not making a claim that the Shadow People live, reside or dwell on or near my property. What I do know is that they wander through at times. There have been several occasions in which we have gotten glimpses of them. Never the prized face-to-face.

There are times, especially at night, when I can tell the Shadow Folks are about. What can be said is if there is a whistle or click and it's verbally answered it will become quiet. Almost like an embarrassed quiet. The Shadow People have had millennia to perfect their camouflage. Like any creature, they adapt to the area they live in.

Until the last few years I had never tried to have a relationship with a giant creature. If you were to ask us to describe how we feel, knowing big hairy guys/gals are wandering the area, well you would get as many answers as there are people in the family.

The problem with a relationship with the gentle creatures of the forest, especially the larger ones, is a basic fear factor. It's built into each and every one of us. There is the fight or flight reaction. I would tell anyone who wants to know more: Take it slow and easy, there is no other way. This is a trust that slowly develops over time. We are talking about a creature that our Creator placed here with us. This creature to my way of thinking is on the same level as those of us without the constant hair shirt. My ancestors believed that to a certain degree if they come forward to you they have a reason, such as an immediate danger to you or your family.

At this point in my relationship I believe that may well be the case. They remain elusive and silent. Habituation any way you want to present it is in fact a relationship. Started by one side or the other, for whatever reason. If you want a relationship with the Shadow People, remember they are intelligent. They are masters of hunting, camouflage, and probably fishing.

I see no harm in gifting, but boundaries need to be established in habituation for the peace of mind and comfort of both sides. Never give what you do not want to be taken. Never set boundaries that you cannot live with. Remember, setting them may not work with intelligent creatures such as the Shadow People. They have had thousands of years to roam about. Just because you don't want one at your back door doesn't mean you have not encouraged this behavior. Think before reacting. Overreaction will not help with any relationship.

I didn't start out to form a relationship with any animal in particular. I certainly never expected to have a tribe visit me in the middle of the night. I do feel that this is a very special gift from them to me that they have chosen our home as a respite at times.

Here's an example of a reaction that I can share. Recently in the middle of the night I was awakened several times to the sounds of scratching on the windows and sides of my home. Annoying to say the least. This continued for several hours throughout the night. And what did the guys want? I have no idea. The scratching noise came to a halt with what sounded like a firm smack and a wounded baboon yelling and running away from the house. What I believe it to be was an errant child "pranking" and Mom becoming tired of this behavior and correcting it.

My reaction was getting up and actually taking the time to try to guess where it was coming from. Each time I turned on a light the noises stopped. As soon as the lights were turned off the noises began again. Did I see Bigfoot standing looking in the window? Nope! I do believe it was the family wandering about. I had left gifts of fruits and nuts for them. I believe they were about because of faint odors that had been detected by my family earlier in the evening.

Our youngest is now eighteen months old. He has a thing he does every chance he gets. He goes to this spot and talks to the window and/or the bushes outside. He doesn't get into anything or bother anything here. He just sits and talks in baby talk to whatever is out there. He waves to it and motions for whatever to come to him.

At first I thought that it was a fluke. Then I started paying attention to him. He does this quite often. He acts the same way he did the night the monkey kids blazed through the yard. He sits and talks and motions to something. He did this that day at nine months old also. Even stranger is when I approach he stops and acts like he is caught doing something he shouldn't. He will not, as long as someone is watching, continue with the baby talk and motions.

I did notice one of Squirt's toy guns is laying out there on the ground. There is a well-worn footpath outside of that window. The interesting part is we rarely us it. The path goes right along the side of the house and out back to the brush and chicken house now. I looked here on Google Earth the other day and you can actually see the footpaths. One of them to the chicken house. Which we have not used in several years. Over three years to be exact.

As I started actually trying to communicate in some manner with the local Shadow People here I tried many things. I have read many on-line conversations with many ideas on communicating with or “baiting” the big guys. A lot of these I dismiss as silly. The silly ideas generally are people who assume that these guys are of lower intelligence than us and must be treated on the level of a child, or a pet.

I fall back on treating the local Shadow People as I would want to be treated. I hate pushy know-it-alls. I avoid them myself. Using how I feel about neighbors and being a neighbor, I started with food and little gifts, which were often taken. I began to add other things: pebbles, feathers, ribbons, all of which have been moved around, relocated or taken.

Then, one day, I wondered how roses would be received. I picked several rosebuds of different sizes and colors and included them with the other items. I found the buds the next day nearby where I had placed them. They were taken apart petal by petal, and left.

A few days later, I awoke and went out to have coffee. I found a trail of pink rose petals to the area where my chair was. At the time I thought, hmmmm, that is odd. Later, I questioned my family about this. No one had done it.

On another morning we found red roses lying on top of the car.

Several weeks after this, I again found a trail of rose petals from the door to the patio. All in all on three different occasions I found a trail of pink rose petals scattered from the front door to the patio.

Our household is taught: "What is done to the least of these is done unto me."

Last night one of the Locals nearly made an appearance. I was sitting on the swing facing my son-in-law who was dropping off my grandchildren. The yard was set up with the wading pool beside the large pool. The kids had already bailed into the pool. Roger was saying good-bye. Sprout [grandson] was in the wading pool and facing towards the house. It was just before dark. I saw movement at the corner of the house. It was a black shadowy figure that darted around from the back towards the front door. The figure moved further out than necessary before diverting back towards the front door.

This was behind Roger's back. Sprout started pointing and yelling, "Granmaa ook ook!" He took a couple of steps forward watching the area where the shadow had moved through. He got out of the pool, walked a few more steps in that direction, then turned around and came over, crawled up and sat down by me on the swing. Son-in-law was fat dumb and happy and missed the whole thing.

This Local was so dark/black that it even stood out against dusk. I am not sure how to describe it other than it was about the size of a medium-sized adult. Broad shoulders. I am not sure if he was hunched. I got the impression he was ducking as he went under the limb of the pine tree.

Later, Dragon Hunter and Fuzzy Wuzzy took some sandwiches out to put in the snack buckets and both were quite unsettled when they came back in. This was about 10:30 pm. Bobbie said that the yard was scary, he saw one of the monkey people out there. He didn't know this one. That for some reason scared him.

Around 11 pm I stepped out for a smoke and on the west side of the house I heard something moving around. It sounded large. It also sounded as if it was picking up a sheet of plywood and dropping it repeatedly. It was not exactly inviting vibes. The geese and dogs were very noticeably quiet.

After the face painting and the hair spray, Dragon Hunter announced that one of the monkey people had been standing off to the north in the bushes watching us. He had seen him. He showed me about where he had been. Same area as last year.

Sprout tried to bolt for the brush a couple of times, pointing and saying, "Dah." He never gets loud when he says, "Dah." It's always said quietly. I don't know what's up with that. He can be quite loud when he is playing.

Today, Sunday, we cooked out. While hubby and my son were talking at the patio, Sprout was on the trampoline playing. He stood up, pointed towards the playhouse, and said, “Dah.” He looked at me and pointed, saying, “Dah” over and over. He walked to the edge of the trampoline as if to get a better look.

Fuzzy Wuzzy asked him where was Addy [another name he uses] and he pointed towards the north. He looked back towards where he had been looking and seemed disappointed. He went back to playing.

Later, around 7 pm, just before it was time for the kids to leave, Sprout and I walked out into the play yard. I had walked away from him, leaving him sitting on the swing. Fuzzy Wuzzy was talking to me and when I turned around Sprout said, “Ook ook!” pointing towards the gifting stump and habitat pile. I couldn't see anything from where I was standing. I watched his expressions as he looked towards the stump. The best way to describe it is recognition, like when you run into an old friend and you just feel happy to see them. Sprout's eyes light up and he smiles and laughs. When he pointed to Dah earlier and now when sitting on the swing looking towards the stump, he shows happiness from the inside out.

I was going through some of my pictures. Sprout and Prissy Princess was looking at them with me. Both Prissy and Sprout were quick to point out the blobs. Sprout pointed to several, clearly saying Dah. Others he just pointed to and looked at me like who is that.

While I was on the phone with Furbaby [a fellow habituator], Sprout came into the kitchen. Furbaby suggested I ask him if Addy and Dah were outside. He climbed up on his bench and began looking out the window. He stared off towards the habitat pile while looking. That look of recognition in his eyes. I didn't see anything out there. Then it was as if he shut down. He has done this for months. When I begin trying to see what he sees he stops looking.

Today while he was in the play yard Magilla and I asked him, “Where is Addy and Dah?” He stopped playing and looked all around. He walked around the yard looking. He was quiet, then he pointed to the front of the property. He stared hard at the cedars and said, “There.” Very plainly said, “There.” I had my back to the cedars and was making an effort not to look where he was looking.

I can't prove it but I think a lot of the sapling bows are just children at play. I know what the researchers say. They try to make it so complicated that there are these big mysteries. I think that the little ones play like children do and at times they ride the trees that are bent while they are playing. There are lots of signs that indicate communication, I won't deny that. I just think that little ones use the trees to play in also.

I have several trees that are bowing and up top in adjacent trees the leaves are missing. These are the same type of leaves that Dragon Hunter and Fuzzy Wuzzy have said they see them eating. They hide well in the trees also. They like to watch us from these places. I have also noticed when one tree is bowed to the point I start paying attention to that area then another tree somewhere else starts bowing.

This is the second time this summer this has happened. Someone short knocks on the front door. Or maybe it is someone taller with a long reach. Twice within the last month someone has knocked on the front door. No one has been there. The first time hubby and Magilla were here and heard it. The first time it happened we thought that Sprout and Fuzzy Wuzzy had arrived. The knock was three then three. Today was a steady knocking on the bottom half of the door. As if someone was trying to get our attention. Magilla and I immediately went out to see what was going on. Nothing absolutely nothing.

I believe they may have those that are from the wilderness and those that are closer to our back doors. That makes the differences in population, evolution habits, and even the way they look. The ones closer to us are on warp drive adapting to us, continually changing. Those in the wilderness are on a much slower pace.

This happened Sunday late afternoon/evening. I was out in the yard. I think better when I am outside. Less distractions in the flowerbeds. Anyway, I looked up and across the yard a large male (probably around 7.5 ft) was standing just outside of the tree line. He was watching me. It was as if he was waiting to get my attention. When I noticed him I watched for a couple of seconds and could even see the white teeth. It was not actually a shock, more of a surprise. I blinked and was wiping sweat from my face. He disappeared.

It only lasted a few seconds.

My impression was he wanted me to know that he had come for his family. They have now gone. I don't know where. I feel better knowing that the female didn't leave alone with little ones. Nothing I can put my finger on. It was as if he was letting me know he had come for his female. He was very black in color. His hair around his head was shoulder length. The body was covered in black hair. His hair appeared short and uniform. Well groomed. His head was round not like a gorilla. Not a huge bulky male more tall and slender. I checked the area where he had been. He had actually stepped from the woods into the yard, there were impressions in the grass.

About three weeks ago, I sent Fuzzy Wuzzy out to turn on the lights around the patio. He came back in and indicated that it was very creepy out. I finally pinned him down. He said he saw a new guy in the yard. Around 9 ft tall. He looked funny because his head was a different color than his body. Fuzzy used the trees this one was near to measure the height. He says it’s too weird to explain, it was like meeting a stranger in the yard. He said when it’s the ones that stay around more it’s just like "Oh hi."

I have some odd things and (as hubby says) “new hillbillies” around. They are just different. They are more tense when they come through here. I believe that Addy left with that male. She may be back in the area but not like she was.... I can't put my finger on things to say for certain, but there is some kind of change or disturbance in patterns. My locals that were comfortable around here seem to be less noticeable. It could be just me also. Addy,

Dah, and the other little guys were around a lot. I would see flashes. Sprout was quick to point them out. Now he isn't pointing them out. He looks for them. He has pointed to a couple of shadows. When asked about them, he don't seem to know them. Not like Addy and Dah. Kinzi says she has seen several that look more monkey than monkey kid. She don't seem to know them either.

On September 24th, while crossing the street, Sprout and his mother were struck by a car, and the boy suffered several injuries, including a skull fracture.

Since Sprout's accident he has not rested very well. He often dreams of the accident. Or I believe he is dreaming about it. He screams in his sleep Help me Help me. Stop it Stop it. During these dreams he is restless. I have to physically restrain him at times. Often it is hard to wake him up. Once he is awake he don't want to sleep again.

On Thursday Oct. 23, he had finally gone to sleep around 11 pm. Around midnight the dreams began. Not able to settle him down I woke him up. After a few minutes I changed the tv to a public tv children's channel and he half watched it, while complaining about his tummy. Then he became excited looking out the front window into the dark (not unusual). He started saying Henry. Henry's here. He pointed out the window and jabbered to the dark and Henry. After doing this. Sprout hopped down and went to the door. He tried to open the door. During this time he was saying, Henry come in the house. Come on in, Henry. He invited Henry to come in several times. I sat watching this, thinking I hope Henry isn't heavy and breaks the porch. A minute or two later Sprout climbed back up to the window looking out. He didn't mention Henry again.

The next night Sprout was again restless and having bad dreams. Around 11 pm I began to hear a humming/singing outside. Really. It was a low sound. As odd as this sounds Sprout settled down and seemed to sleep peacefully. I don't know how long the humming went on. In the wee hours of the morning Sprout became restless again. I barely recall holding him and the humming beginning again. This was the third time I have heard the humming now. There has not been any wind when I hear the humming. Or that is to say I don't observe the trees swaying in the wind. I have investigated around the house looking for some sort of device that the wind could blow through to make the sound, should somehow I have missed noticing the wind. I have not found anything. I can say if it's a hairless person humming they are either bundled up or freezing their butts off. I have not attempted to record anything in a while. I have debated each time I hear the humming on trying to sneak the recorder out. I have decided against this each time. I somehow suspect the humming will come to an end.

This evening Sprout came out on the porch. He flipped on the porch light and called to Dah. He called several times softly. Then he yelled it very loudly a half a dozen more times or so. He acted very excited while calling for him. Then he went back into the house. A couple of minutes later he came busting out the door a second time and said, KeeKee! KeeKee's here! He looked around as if expecting her to step up to the porch. He went and got a sack of cat food and proceeded to pour a pile on the porch. After making a mess of the cat food he picked it up and put it into a bowl and proceeded to tell the cats they couldn't have it.

[Author's Note: In 2009, researcher Pat Rance visited this site and obtained middle-of-the-night eyeshine video at the edge of the yard. This footage is included in "A Figure by the Bench: Oklahoma Habituation Site," posted on YouTube, as is the toy dragon that was flipped over, and the habituator's voice describing her photography practice.]

3. Iowa

Bonnie is sixty-one years old and has lived in the area since birth. Three generations of her family have experienced Sasquatch encounters here. Like many other habituators, she has long suffered from health trouble, including severe respiratory problems. Feeling chronically unwell can predispose people to a more vigilant attitude, a certain stillness, an outsider or misfit status, and more awareness of their surroundings, perhaps because they are forced to slow down, to live one day at a time, and not to get so caught up in the average person's busy, distracted stream of existence. Fair warning: The incident involving the horse in February 2005, below, is very disturbing to read and demonstrates that, as is true in our own species, certain Sasquatch—particularly young, unaffiliated males—are capable of violence.

1957-1966

I was seven years old and taking my four-year-old brother to the outhouse. He ran on ahead and then came back saying there was bear in the outhouse. When we got there, there was no bear inside, so while my brother was using the toilet, I was swinging on the door and that's when I saw it, standing behind the outhouse. I remember thinking it was a really big one, whatever it was. It was a male and just stood there looking at me.

I never heard of other sightings in the area and never told kids at school what I was seeing. Heck, my half-brothers saw them too but we never told our parents. We knew better: When my little brother told our father that he'd seen a bear in the outhouse, he got whooped. Our father would knock you through the floor if you said anything like that.

I was never scared of them. I didn't think of myself as lucky, either. They were just there. I've always whistled, for the animals, and young Sas would come closer.

We'd go berry-picking with Grandma. We'd start out in the morning, and pick berries till night. Gallons of them. And they'd be lying nearby and we never talked about it. But she knew, you could see it on her face, but she'd act like they weren't there. She never once acknowledged them. Well, once she did say there were old Indians around, and to be careful of them. I *never* felt threatened.

I used to walk on top of the barbed-wire fences. And so I think that's where the hairy kids learned it, from me. I'd see them walking on the barbed wire. Their feet are real thick and calloused.

The time I heard one scream I was sixteen, and I wondered what was going on. I walked around till I found some men wearing sheets and sacrificing animals. I figured they were KKK. The scream was very high-pitched and loud, and you could tell the men had heard it too because they were looking around nervously. There was just the one scream, though. I lay there in the grass for a while and watched them sacrifice a dog, but I was smart enough to know that a young girl should not show herself to these men.

One time our neighbor's bulls got into it. There was a Hereford bull on one side of the fence, an Angus bull on the other. And one got to shoving the corner post and it come loose, so the rail come down and the two bulls started going at each other, really seriously, biting and stuff. At about that time, a Sas come out of nowhere, in the woods, and come up to where they were at, maybe fifty feet away from the bulls. I saw it. It opened its mouth and screamed at them. It sounded like a monkey, like that loud chimpanzee scream. It got their attention to where the bulls took off, it scared them. I think the Sas was saying, "Okay, I've had enough of this." Then he just went back into the forest.

1994-Present

My husband has never seen one but somehow he seems connected to them in his mind. Once, he told me exactly where they stay at. And seven or eight times, I've heard him talking in his sleep, having a conversation, and I'll go look out the window and sure enough, there one will be standing in the yard, twenty feet away. Michael will just be talking like a normal conversation, sometimes mumbling that I can't make out, and sometimes…you're not going to believe this…but he talks like the Sasquatch in the "Sierra Sounds" audio. Sometimes the next morning he'll tell me he dreamed he was talking to one, and I just say, "Oh really?"

He doesn't seem to have a burning desire to see one, and so it don't bother me one way or another. It's like he's got two different minds.

One night he was sleeping and said, "They run my dog through with a spear." I found out later from his sister that when they were kids they found their dog with a thick stick all the way through him.

The alarm on his truck will go off every night at about two AM. He always leaves goodies in there. They tried to open the door and the alarm would go off, and one of us would have to go out and shut it off.

The little ones will come up close to the house at night. I've put out pieces of granite for them to sit on, two foot by two-and-a-half foot, because they always used to break the wooden benches. They'll come up and harass us some. I've put wind chimes up, so if I hear a wind chime I'll know what it is. They'll tap on the glass or touch the screen. I have one that hollers, "Bonnie! Bonnie! Bonnie!" And I'll shout back, "Be quiet!"

They will follow my daughter-in-law and my son everywhere around this place. He's forty-one. He's been seeing them since he was a kid. The first time he was in the fifth grade and he told me about it. I told him it was a bear, even though he said it was walking on two legs. I didn't want to scare him. When he was older, he had one grab him while he was splitting wood. It just come and grabbed him, hugged him. This didn't last very long. He screamed and it run off.

I think this is the same one that put his hand on my daughter when she was fifteen, on her back. She said the hand stretched from the base of her skull to halfway down her back. She and her brother were out checking traps, on a Friday night after he got home from work. When he turned on the flashlight to go down the hill to the river, it quit working. So she stayed there at the top and he went down, he didn't need no light. He wasn't gone but fifteen minutes, and when my daughter felt the hand, she thought at first that he was playing a trick on her, but when she hollered he answered from way down by the river. She'd seen them before, but she was like in denial.

One time her brother, my son, went camping out in the winter, and the next morning I go down to check on him and there were Sas tracks all around him.

At first I was scared for my grandkid. Down the hill we have what's called a junk pit, and I remembered seeing a Sasquatch down there. I said to my five-year-old grandson, "Stay away from there or the Junk Pit Monster will getcha." Then one day he come up and said, "I went down there and I talked to the monster and he told me he wouldn't hurt me."

My daughter (the same one who got touched) was still kind of in denial, but she come over for coffee one morning and left about ten o'clock, and I heard that whistle and I knew they were up close to the house. My daughter gets down the road and calls me on her cell phone, and tells me she saw a big old red one on the other side of the barn. I'd seen him before. They're so common, it's like seeing dogs.

I used to leave them sweet feed all the time, but then things got tough and we couldn't afford it anymore. So I told them I was sorry but that we could hardly get what we need for ourselves and the horses. One morning, I went out to the barn to water the horses, and there was a deer leg.

I always leave stuffed animals out and they move them around. The car keys from my son's truck were moved into our boat one time. Stuff like that. I have a little wagon to haul firewood, and I never know where I'm going to find that wagon.

They mimic our voices too, all the time, to mess with us. The grandkids'll say, "We heard you hollering for us," and I'll say, "Oh…yeah." Again, I don't want to scare them.

We used to love to ride horses in the moonlight, but then I had my knee replaced and it hurt to ride, so I started riding my ATV. One night it was a full moon and I wanted to go out. I stepped off the porch and felt "the fear" that everyone talks about, and this was something I'd never experienced before. So I just stood there looking around, and all of a sudden across the field it looked like a whole bunch of bicycle reflectors moving along, and evidently they wanted me to stay out of their way.

Once, I bought this homemade doll with buttons sewed on for eyes, and I thought, I'll take it down there, because I knew where the little ones were at, at the mouth of the creek where it feeds into the lake. First day, nothing happened, I went down and checked. Second day, I went down there and the eyes were gone and the material, like nylon, looked like it had been cut in two circles. Their fingernails are very sharp. And the two eyes were laid inside a fish carcass. Looks like they thought they belonged on a fish instead of a babydoll. They do lots of little funny things like that. We left out flutes, little recorders, first showed them how to play it. And pretty soon we heard them being played in the middle of the night, down in the cornfield.

One Sunday afternoon, my three grandkids and I was out behind the barn a bit and lying on some big bales of hay that were lined up next to the fence row. The two girls and I were on one bale and my grandson on the other. We were all watching a mama fox and her babies with the binoculars. As the girls and I were watching the fox my grandson says, "Hey Grandma," and hands me the binoculars. "Look, another Junk Pit Monster is catching deer." As I put the binoculars up to my eyes I seen five deer standing over by the junk pit grazing on the clover pasture. I seen this large sorrel-colored Sas coming out of the tree line. I watched this critter run up alongside that deer and grab the deer by the underside of the neck and bend the head back to its butt. Must of broke its back. He carried it off into the timber without missing a step. It was all done and over with, within two minutes. As the thing ran up to the deer it was on all fours. After grabbing it and bending its neck back then it walked off on two feet carrying the deer on its right shoulder.

Last part of October 2002

I had decided to go for one of my early morning walks and I headed out across the pasture. Following me were four horses, two dogs and a cat. They go on most of my walks as they are my buddies. Now I was talking to them and we were walking along having a good time when we come upon the edge of the timber. All of a sudden the horses spun around and took off with the cat and one dog with them. All that was left was Boss and me. He was looking over at the timber and did this low growl thing. I looked and all I could see was a shadow. Huge shadow on the timber. We were about thirty-five feet from the edge of the timber. I hadn't remembered the shadow being there before and as I looked down at the dog with his hair standing up and back to the shadow it had moved ways to the right. I decided it was time to go back as Boss wouldn't if I didn't and this thing was too darn big to mess with even for him.

That evening it was almost completely dark and I was at the gate out by the barn and petting the old mare and talking to her. The mastiff mix was up close to me and Boss was not far from the front porch. All of a sudden this huge thing ran by me after the dogs. As I turned Boss was gone and this big hairy thing was right on the other dog's tail, close behind. They all disappeared in the timber.

Fifteen or twenty minutes later Boss showed up and wanted in the house. The other dog was never seen again.

Mid-February 2005

It was about 11 AM and I was washing my back door window panes. It had been a very warm winter and not much snow. Not typical of Iowa in February. It was about forty to forty-five degrees outside. A few days before, it had snowed a light dusting. There is a lot that I call the feeder lot out back of the barn. At the far end of it there is a gate that you go through into a little patch of timber that is about sixty yards long and on into another pasture. Now back in July of 2004 I had rescued a filly that was almost fifteen hands tall and weighed in at about a hundred pounds. She was just walking bones. Now as a new-comer she was the low dog on the pecking order. I had a big four-year-old gelding, an older mare who ran things, a year-old filly, and the rescued filly. I was just washing those windows when the old mare came to the gate and screamed at me. It was a high-pitched shrill noise is why I say screamed at me. I threw on my coat and grabbed my camera. I thought Big Cat. As I get out to the feed lot I see the gelding walking on his back legs and biting at the air with his nose holes flared bigger that I knew they could ever be flared. The year-old filly was just running around in circles and making high-pitched noises. I noticed the rescued filly wasn't in sight. As I walked into the feed lot the mare gets on my left and the gelding gets on my right. I wasn't walking but not full-out running. Now those two horses stayed right with me and never got more than a few inches from my body. We are heading down to the gate that leads into the timber patch looking for the missing filly. Just as we got to the gate there in the timber part about twenty feet in was what I called the Monkey Man. It had that filly and was raping her.

She was on her front legs but her butt was pulled to this Monkey Man and she was almost in a sitting position. The Monkey Man had ahold of her shoulders. As it seen me and looked me straight in the eyes for a good three or four seconds it let her loose making three scratches down each of her sides from chest to hips. She had been trying to get loose and when he let her go she stumbled and could hardly get to me and the other two horses as she was shaking too badly. Then the smell came and I started coughing. It was like an asthma attack. Those eyes were very small and black, mean and wild-looking. It felt that he looked to my soul. That's when I started shaking like the horse. I did not move until he did. He just casually turned and strolled off, taking big strides and swinging his arms.

I turned and the two horses were standing right with me and the rescued filly had made it a little farther past them. She stood there and waited for all of us. Still shaking, the both of us. I started talking with her and got ahold of her and took her inside the barn where I kept all my meds for the horses. She had blood running down the backs of her legs almost to her hooves. She had the scratches down both sides. I took a rag and a bucket of water and washed and dried her down. I took the tube of triple antibiotics that was in a tube and squeezed it into a syringe then put that in her vulva. I put another kind of salve that my grandmother taught me to make on the scratches on her sides. Gave her a shot of penicillin, some food and water, and went to the house. I could not quit shaking myself. I thought, Who the hell do I call that would believe such a story? So I called the bird watcher. He and his father came out within fifteen minutes.

I was sitting on the front porch, shaking and making a sketch of what I saw. I was coughing and having a hard time breathing. I took them down to where the crime happened and told them I was going to check on the horse and go to bed. I went to bed and slept for the better part of three days. My husband said I told him it felt like I had been poisoned.

When I woke up after the third day I thought it had been a dream. So I went out and looked the horse over and sure enough she had scratches all the way down on both sides. She seemed to be ok and we went on as usual.

Two weeks later my son brings a girlfriend to visit and she had a twelve-year-old daughter who had short dark hair like the Monkey Man. Up until then none of these horses seemed to have a mean bone in their bodies. That girl tried to pet the gelding and he bit her, almost biting her ear off. Much more and he would have. I still was having problems breathing and went to the local doctor. They gave me antibiotics and said I had bronchitis. They gave me three rounds and it still wasn't any better. Then I went into the hospital with pneumonia. It took me a good six months altogether to get to feeling better. Though my breathing has never gotten back to normal.

By granddaughter Kimberly, eleven years old, September 12th, 2006

Last year about eight o'clock in the evening when we were staying in my grandma's camper, I was going to go to her house on the other side of the barn. I had just came out of the camper and was behind the barn when I looked up to see a Bigfoot. He was standing just on the other side of the fence and was slightly turned though he was looking right at me. He was about ten yards from me. He had dirty gray long straight hair and big lips. He had a big wide nose. I wasn't scared but I was freaked out. He smelt weird, a nasty rotten smell. Part of his hair was messy and part of it wasn't. He was as tall as my grandma's walls in her house. He seemed to just say Hi to me but it wasn't in words. He looked like a monkey he was so hairy. But also like a man with a beard. He didn't seem mean at all. But I just turned around and went back into the camper and told my brother if he wanted to get a movie from Grandma he would have to go get it himself. I didn't tell anyone because at first I thought I had imagined it. Besides that, my mom and brother don't believe in the Bigfoot and they would have made fun of me or Mom would have said Grandma is brain-washing me. My birthday is September 21st so I was ten years old at the time. I finally told Grandma last night as I know she is telling the truth. She showed me a drawing of another Bigfoot on a book and mine looked like this only his face wasn't as dark. It was only half that dark.

Kimberly continued, August 14th, 2007

My grandma, me and my cousin Brenda went out to talk with them. My grandma yelled "Whooo!" It didn't take long before four of them came up to the front of the house and we stood on the porch and talked with them. Grandma told me how there would be a dead zone (all quiet) and there was when they came up. One chirped at us, one popped his teeth at us. I did not feel scared at all. We watched one play with the barn door and make it squeak as it opened and shut the door for about a foot. Grandma then asked them if they were hungry and if they would like a treat. One said yes. Grandma said it was a male. Me and Brenda heard him say yes. Since it was so late, about midnight, Grandma said she wasn't making pancakes at that time of night for anyone. She went in and took four slices of bread and laid them on a plate and poured maple syrup on the bread. She told them to eat it and if they wanted more they would have to leave the plate on the porch. She set the plate on the top of her jeep right in the middle of the top. Grandma, Brenda and me sat out on the porch and just talked to each other. We saw shadows of two feet on the other side of the jeep only it was from underneath the jeep. The plate disappeared. We could see it plain as it was a white plate. Grandma's other car was sitting behind the jeep and we saw a shadow block out the light that shined on the hood of that car. So we got tired and went into the house and this morning found the plate back on top of the jeep but it was at the other side and at the back of it on the roof. They ate the whole piece that was the heel and part of another only it was just picked out in the middle. They must of not liked it as they didn't put the plate on the porch.

Back to Bonnie, August 2009

I have granddaughters who visit here, and I'm very careful when they're on their monthlies. They all know that they aren't to go out by themselves after dark. There's one that I call Baby Boy, he was obsessed with my granddaughter Brenda, and you could hear him calling "Brenda…Brenda" from the woods. Day or night. He left her gifts in this one spot, and she left little colored rocks that she bought at the Dollar Store. All my kids have done gifts with them. So he left seven of these magnetic stones, I have no idea where he got them. They weren't like the polished ones you see. These were rough in places and rubbed smooth in places.

Closest I've ever been is about four or five feet away. This was in the summertime. I was talking to my girlfriend on the front porch deck, and I'm talking on the phone and all of a sudden he just popped up in front of me, the old gray one. The deck is about eight feet off the ground, and I could see his head and shoulders and chest. He looked silver in the moonlight. His hair was really fine, like a collie dog's. I couldn't mention it to my girlfriend, so I'm talking to her just like normal but looking at him. He was cocking his head back and forth, listening, looking at me like "What are you talking into?" He was so close and the light was so good I could see his pupils, and they were like cats' eyes.

I have no desire to shoot video of them. I wouldn't want someone taking pictures of me without my permission.

4. New York State

Jerry is a thirty-year-old man who lives with his parents. As a teenager, he was hit by a car and suffered a brain injury that still affects him. He has been having experiences with Sasquatch since childhood. I have been corresponding with him since November, 2006, and was able to visit him twice, in June and December of 2007; this chapter represents both our viewpoints.

May 1985

He was six years old the first time.

"When I met them I had peanut butter and jelly sandwiches," Jerry told me, "and as I remember it they stayed close to me but divvied the pieces up between them. Remember we were way back in they woods so there was nothing for them to run and hide from, it was just me. When they finished what was my lunch but gave to them instead they wanted more but that was it. So [the main male] Miget and his woman—I call her Momma—seen that I gave them my food and fed me some of theirs like some berries we went foraging for. They tasted good from what I remember but I knew I was going to have dinner waiting for me when I went home."

For the next twenty-four years, Jerry has kept up consistent and loyal contact with this same group of Sasquatch. Because they live in a severely limited tract of land, boxed in by suburban residences, he has steadfastly kept their secret, knowing that any leak could cause their ouster, if not their destruction. They have subsisted here, in fact, since before Jerry's great-grandfather first interacted with them in the 1950s, and these accounts were passed down through the generations.

The more he has come to trust me, through our correspondence, the more he has felt comfortable in sharing with me of his past with these *people.* “I like to refer to them as people, not animals.” He thinks there were “many races of *homo sapiens* roaming the earth at one time but many of them went extinct. I just like to think that this is one race that slipped through the cracks and remained on the wild side of things.”

He has also long known that he’d like to find a trustworthy researcher to take along to the site, to help him to officially document their reality (without exposing their home territory), to establish it definitively within mainstream science, and thus to get the wheels turning toward legal protection for the species.

I agreed not to breathe a word of their location, and I have not. That they have managed to survive without discovery in a constricted stronghold of forest—a forest that, albeit thick, comprises just seven square miles—speaks better than any other case I know to their uncanny stealth and adaptability.

“I mean, lots of people know they’re back there, even my great-grandpa knew about them and told me about his experiences with them before he passed. He even called them his friends. I just think it's kind of weird how I got to know the same family I like to call the Migets. And it's not certain that they just stay in [name of forest]. I'm sure they go other places, but I know they like to stay close to the stream for water.

“I can't say how many are back there but there are at least five or six that I know of. There can very well be more because they are too unsure or bashful of us men. When I first met Miget, the patriarch or leader, his father was still alive and he was very old but didn't look like it through his actions. They are a very peaceful group of people but very curious of us and at the same time even more scared of us. They are caring of each other and protective of things they take care of. They are even more curious of our foods and simple luxuries like hair combs.

"One time when I was fly fishing, Miget's boy—I call him Junior—walked up behind me and scared me because I didn't hear him till he was right behind me and he was all fuzzy because it was March so he still had his winter coat, but he was only four to five feet tall I guess you could consider him a little guy. He was very uncertain and a little offensive but very curious and just like that he disappeared when I turned my back to check my line.

"The few times when they vocalized for me, I could make out some of our words strangely enough. I hate to sound like a delusional crazy person with all the info I've come forward with but it's what I know. These are wild people we're dealing with and with all their humanness they're still very wild. It's kind of spooky when you think of it or when the situation occurs.

"If someone don't have the right look they won't trust or understand what you say through the simple sign language along with slow talking. They also understand when you speak like them, it comes natural when the moment arises, it's weird. There's no need to practice. The feelings they feel conjure up in you are like a link to our common past.

"One time, I brought my friend back there when cutting school and we were walking about a quarter mile back and I looked to my side and there was Junior. Just sitting there with a grin on his face looking at me like an old friend being reacquainted. My school friend started shaking uncontrollably and ran back to school. After Miget came into sight with his brother we had a visit for a while and I went back to school myself. When I ran into my friend in the hall he was so shaken up he forgot what happened. Which is good because I think that happens to a bunch of people because it is so unbelievable that their brain doesn't register it. Just like the Indian folklore they say that they have magic and control you.

"I'm not really out for self-glorification, but want the truth to be known before it's too late or introduced in the wrong way. But you want to know what my theory is? These people are going to be here after man is extinct. They'll be using our structures in a simplified way. Like a highway overpass would be their idea of a home, for instance, and so forth.

"Among the Migets, the female has something beautiful about her. You can tell she's a woman by her figure of course plus the way she walks and by the look in her eyes, it's gentler. It's definitely different than the guys. That's once you get them to feel comfortable. The guys have a build that will make the world's strongest man look like a little girl. The ladies are built and strong too but different if that makes sense.

"They are like us but they groom each other and they got wild eyes if you look them straight on at first, then they relax. They're like a married couple, they bicker and everything. Plus I didn't want to share this because I didn't feel you would believe me, but they had a baby. When I was a kid. I seen him the second time I was taken back in the woods. I might be the only human to see a baby Bigfoot. Very cute, he looked like a newborn maybe a foot and a half from head to toe or two feet maybe.

"They had him in a piece of cloth they scavenged from somewhere. I forgot to tell you when I seen Missy [a younger female] the first time, Miget came out of the woods about fifty feet away and called for her like *come on let's go you*, that was the tone. So there's Miget, Momma, Sissy, Junior, and Little Brother. Plus Miget's brother who I call Uncle Bugout, because he loses his temper. I'm just amazed how those little ones do alright in the winter. This particular family is lucky they have our pollution and waste to pick from for a baby blanket if that's what you want to call it. It makes you feel bad when you think how poor they are but happy.

"Oh, Miget. He was a very big boy since I first knew him. I can remember standing in front of him and having to tilt my head totally back towards the sky to see the top of him. It's still like that today. Miget has been at least ten feet for as long as I've known him, and three or four feet wide, a true powerhouse. He can clear a path running full speed."

Visiting Jerry

We meet on warm June afternoon teeming with goldfinches and deafening insect life. Our plan is to spend the day and the night in the woods, though I must confess that even after months of copious email exchanges, of apparently sincere testimony from this man, I'm still feeling only about 50/50 on his ultimate credibility; after all, what he is asking me to buy into—in terms of his childhood experiences—seems far too good to be true.

Add to this, now, the fact that although Jerry spent his youth (and knew "the Migets") *downstate,* he claims to have made contact, over this past winter and spring, with yet *another* family group up here, hundreds of miles from the first.

This fact does not, however, strike him as remotely strange; his contention is that these people live in most forests, but that human beings do not, as a rule, have the foggiest notion, much less any aptitude for outreach.

Jerry is just about my height, six feet, heavy-set, with bad knees that cause him to sway back and forth a little when he walks. He works in a machine shop, where he puts together transmission housings. On weekends and occasional days off, he is free to spend quiet hours inside the forest, just two miles from town. What strikes one first is how soft-spoken and down-to-earth he is; nothing mystical or rash passes his lips, and his body-language is understated, facial expressions even humdrum, the opposite of what one might expect after hearing his mind-boggling stories.

As he leads me through tall grasses on top of a high clearing, he's more interested in agriculture than in Sasquatch, pointing out the various farmers' fields, telling me their names, and whether or not they've fallen behind schedule in the season's first haying. He clearly enjoys the look of these swatches of land arrayed below us in the valley.

On the downslope, we approach and pass through the tree line, leaving the goldfinches and bright sunlight behind. It takes us no more than ten minutes, once inside the woods, to make our way over roots, fallen trees, and along informal fernways to Jerry's hide-out, a simple but effective lean-to he's constructed out of sturdy branches and pine boughs.

The very moment we arrive—and I mean the *very* moment, even before we can sling off our backpacks—a single, distinct wood knock pierces through the thick trees, coming from our west, maybe seventy yards away. Jerry looks at me. "I told you so."

I have to laugh, from pleasure in hearing this, and because he certainly *has* told me, in great detail. We set up a sparse camp—thermoses of coffee, collapsible chairs, candy bars, a candle set on a rock—and then spend four hours alternately talking and meditatively listening. It's breezy, my heart's bruised from a fresh, treacherous breakup with the mother of my child, and sunspots swirl over the forest understory.

What follows is a blend of Jerry's words from our conversation this afternoon and from his emails to me over the past six months.

I start by conceding that during all my BFRO expeditions, and certainly in my solo time in the woods, I've never gotten such an unmistakable overture as the wood knock we just heard.

"Maybe you're not listening enough once they know you're there. They'll give you one really soft knock. That means you're in their sight and you don't even know it. It sounds crazy but you have to become an animal in your head.

"Remember, you're going into *their world.* They have super senses as it is, so you shouldn't have to over-extend yourself to get their attention. Keep it simple. I feel the BFRO might be too loud when they're on expeditions. When you think about it they already know we're reckless and loud as a race. That's why they stay away altogether. The researchers stay in a crowd out there. Why fill the woods with a bunch? Simple sounds, little whoops go a long way too. That's why they aren't yelling out more as well. They don't have to, they already got great hearing. I'm the kind of guy that sets off in the woods by myself. I don't like talking out here unless I try to talk with one of them, like last week when he threw a rock at a tree by me. Then I talked calmly but excited. Yup, keep it simple. They get spooked about people to begin with.

"They can feel when a person's spirit is good and means good, that's why I've gotten this far. They're just watching out for themselves right now, that's what's happening. You know this all seems simple but the biggest aspect of this besides them is to share good information for their sake and not to let people see them the wrong way but to love and respect them as the fathers of the woods."

Again and again, he stresses the indispensable importance of sincerity.

"Once they know who you are they aren't offended or threatened. I think I just lucked out or maybe I have a peaceful look in my eyes or maybe it's because I am a big guy or I look and act like them, ha. I do enjoy spending lots of time in the woods too, maybe I'm being checked out from a distance and their curiosity brings them in.

"I have to tell you about my experience in the Poconos. When I lived there ten years ago sometimes there would be a thump or tap on the wall of my house on the wall behind my TV at night. I would be wondering what it was so I went outside one night with my dog and out of the woods came a seven-to-eight-foot teenage male. My dog Jack got between us, and it almost attacked him but I walked up to my dog and started petting him and saying good boy, with a calm voice. The male looked in amazement as Jack calmed down, then I started to play with my dog and he seemed to understand. I could swear that he said 'Jack' too in a pleased voice after I introduced him."

This is the type of thing, of course, that stretches one's credulity. Jerry relates the anecdote as if he's telling me about some innocuous street-corner encounter.

Another such: When he was a kid, he was once able to touch the lower back of a female before she moved off. "I remember her hair was coarse and real *oily*. I guess that's how they stay dry in the rain, the water runs right off."

Winter Work

He writes me near-daily updates on his careful process of outreach to the Upstate locals, when he first established their presence.

January 12th, 2007: "I had a gnarly day out in the woods my friend. I went for a walk four or so hours ago and just got home. I brought my homemade club for wood-knocking. I was knocking the whole way back on that road I was telling you about where I seen the bear, they're asleep now I'm sure. But I also know there are Migets in the area because of the deep woods and past experience.

"Well, I went down this path leading deep into the woods. I gave a power pole a good crack before I left into the woods. I wasn't too far when I heard it, a huge thud coming from across the valley in a deep patch of woods I could pick out. Along with another crack far deeper and more powerful than I could ever make. Well I kept on my way out there into the wilderness. I kept on finding things to beat on and finally found a nice rock with a good flat side. I stayed in one spot so I could listen with a vantage point over two valleys to hear and see over the woods and farm fields, and so they could hear me. I was getting responses now only with far-off knocks in the woods. I was knocking my club on the rock and gave it a rest. Then I couldn't place it but there was definitely something on two legs walking around me somewhere with big feet. I could tell from the sound the snow made when it packed, it was so cool. I made contact, not how I wanted though.

"I wanted to stay out there and make a visual and even a close-up encounter. Oh yeah, I also seen some foot prints on the seasonal road on my way back. I couldn't say how big or how fresh because they were wind eroded, but they sure did look big."

I pointed out, by email, that most people wouldn't be able to stay out for hours with their face exposed.

"No, I like the cold. My jaw was hurting when I got back. With the wind it was like a sandblaster out there. But about the knocks. I couldn't believe it at first. I figured someone was chopping wood. But that was a thud. I also heard a vocalization, a whoop with a little monkey chatter. It didn't last for more than a few seconds, twice.

"At first, the knocking came from my east then after a while it came from my west. Which means it was trying to locate me. Then the footsteps packing the snow put it in stone for me. The steps sounded like they were within fifty feet of me. That means he or she could see me but I couldn't see them. In that state of mind looking around to figure out where the sound was coming from, you could easily overlook a perfectly camouflaged figure in a dark woods, plus I was down in the ravine. It might have kept back once the wind really started up and blew my scent toward it and it figured out I was a man. Otherwise it might have just walked up to me until I came into its vision. I was hidden in the ravine good enough to not be seen. There were snow banks tucking me in."

January 21st, 2007: "I spent about, oh, three or four hours out there today and just got back five minutes ago. I headed down the hill on the dirt road and went east by the pond. I was only on that path a few seconds and seen a set of tracks come out of the woods and head down the path, I couldn't tell what direction, they weren't fresh. They didn't have a big stride, so I figured it was a young one. If it was a human what were they doing out that far and why coming out of the deep woods like that? Then again what was I doing out that far? So I said to myself, this is the spot to try today. So I took a good swing with my Bigfoot club three times. It was a few minutes before I got a response far away but I did, ha. Once again the knocks got closer than a mile and changed location. They were trying to find me, oh shit. Then from the next tree line over a half mile away I seen a head poke out from behind a tree and look from side to side I seen its shoulders too. That was north of me. I gave another good set of knocks and got a response right away, no vocals just knocks today. Then I started to think about the pine forest behind me and the fact that they like sneaking up on you. I remember this from [downstate location]. Even when you do see them it's always like the first time you met, you always get spooked because they just appear or sneak up, it's just a weird feeling. They stare at you with those wild eyes and neither of you know what to think of each other.

"Anyway, back to today. I knew this young one from the ridge across the way seen me so it was a matter of time. It was only a six- or seven-footer by the looks of it. I kept on knocking at least every five minutes. Now I knew I was in the middle of a family, because I was hearing knocks all around me in at least three or four locations. Then I heard a knock maybe shit at least within a hundred yards, with the limb he was using snapping. I knocked right away and just like I figured they were surrounding me from behind so I kept looking over my shoulder once in a while playing along. Then I had to turn around altogether because I heard him break a tree limb off a tree. I studied for a second and there he was, a big boy.

You know Chris maybe you're right I might have some magic in me they're drawn to. Well there he was very still now because I had my eyes set on him almost like he was hunting or stalking I should say. He had a look on his face like what the hell does this guy want, it looked kind of pissed off in a studying kind of way. I started making humming sounds, then I surprised him with a whoop. His face changed altogether like oh that's who has been whooping outside of town. Then he looked to the west in the forest, a thick forest I might add. So he was with a buddy, making facial expressions in a calm manner like it's ok he's a friend or something like that. This guy is huge, at first when I glanced his way I thought it was a fallen tree or a stump, then I made out the face. He was crouched up, hunched over. (Solid.) He has a wide black face and fur. A tall forehead and a cone-like dome on top. Big shoulders and huge legs from what I could make out. He was pretty far off, maybe five hundred feet. He was looking around him now a lot. He had no reason to run I was in the middle of nowhere on his turf. So I started eating some peanut butter crackers I packed in my pocket and offering to him. So I ate the whole pack and said mmm every bite, while smooching kisses. Everything understands smooches. I left an open pack in two tree limbs high up for him to get.

"I wasn't that surprised by what happened today, a major milestone. I figure little steps now that they know who I am, I'll be back. The crackers just helped to tell them I'm a good guy.

"So I took a piss and left swaying my arms and looking back every couple of hundred feet, waving back. I knew they would be looking or eating the crackers. I feel all giddy inside when I think of it now. Now that I give it a good figure in my recollection, he had to have been five hundred to eight hundred feet away. I should have left more crackers. Well there's always tomorrow."

January 25th, 2007: "I went out there at 11:00 am and back to the same spot. Again, it only took about fifteen minutes to get a knock response. I think I found their winter hangout, a nice thick spruce forest."

"Still," I say today, the following summer, long hours since we heard that first welcoming knock, "fifteen minutes can feel like an eternity."

"Two things that keep people from making contact," Jerry instructs me, "are impatience and disbelief.

"Okay, so I started out at the top of the hill whooping my way in. I got there and was knocking. The knocks started back and they weren't just tree trunks expanding with the coldness. A big knock out a half mile followed with one close to my east. The sound of thumping snow pack again around me. I couldn't see Buddy run but I knew it was him by the sound. Branches crunching now and again by mistake or just a spurt of quick movement. But today he wasn't where I seen him last time so that means I wasn't seeing things last time, just checking myself. I looked north and seen a head and shoulders that moved between vertical tree trunks maybe a half mile across the field up the hill."

"Wow," I say, "a half *mile*?"

"Yeah. People don't look far enough, hell they don't even look a *quarter* as far as they should when they're out. It happens a lot. You just have to know what silhouettes to look for and be able to tell the difference between tree trunks and legs, arms and fur. I tell ya, Man, we're dealing with the Abominable Special Forces. These guys are good at what they do.

"So I started humming very nicely. The knocks continued but only north of me after the ones to the east and west within a few hundred feet. Then a while later I heard a hum grumble very low in tone in the woods behind me followed by a big knock to the right of me which was where he was. Big knocks deeper in the woods a half mile to the northeast going deeper and closer. I finally caught on. They wanted me to go deeper in the woods, too, so I did. I went west on this path a half mile out of sight of the other area when I heard a burst of movement from where he was to keep an eye on me. I found a stream and stopped and hung up a bag of apples and crackers and a banana, since I found a peel a while back. Oh yeah he only took one cracker from the other day, you could see he ripped the bag open and dropped it in the snow. Also, I found a set of some tracks with an at least a six-to-seven-foot stride downhill. I had to do a split to make one step.

"I was hearing something behind me, thumping, no reason to worry they're just checking you out. I had the feeling that if they could only draw me out deeper they could attempt to approach me. It felt like at least six individuals around me. One kept knocking and would go deeper, knock, go further knock, and then come all the way back and knock in the same area. I would whoop and get a single knock in return immediately. I was in my chair and looking north towards the food bag knocking my chair leg.

"When I heard something over my shoulder I took a look and out of nowhere a huge knock came from in front of me when I wasn't looking. I instantly responded with a loud (nice) whoop and got out of my chair, and a rock was thrown at a tree a hundred feet in front of me. That means you're not welcome I've heard, but they just don't know me yet. I feel they're testing my reaction, so I stayed friendly. Then there was a vocal from what I thought was a youngster who couldn't hold himself back out of curiosity. Not a big one just a bleep or a boop. It's funny because when I'm home thinking, I get a bit spooked about what could happen with a nine-hundred-pound wildman, but when I get out there that all changes. It's like we're both playing opposite sides of the same game board, both very curious and very unsure."

Jerry points to a branch that forms part of the lean-to opening. "I came back here one day to find a single blade of green grass just hanging there. And remember, this was *February*."

It's twilight now, and it comes to our attention that we're famished, unwilling to follow our loose plan of fasting all night. Hiking back out to town, though, our dim foresight suddenly turns to luck. A ridge above us, probably two hundred feet away across a green and yellow field, begins to ring out with voices. Just two, but nonhuman, calling back and forth. It's a cross between a howling and the long sustain of great big bells, and since there are no wolves (or, okay, *virtually* no wolves) in Upstate New York, and since this vocalization contains, anyway, zero of the yipping uptake or the group-choral quality of coyotes, nothing but the high song portion itself, and since it comes from the very area where this straightforward young man has claimed to see and hear "them" for months, I feel my belief level shoot from 50% to 85%.

"Captivating, isn't it?" says Jerry. "I think it's a female and a juvenile, a couple hundred yards apart. That's what it seems like to me. Hope you're getting this," he says, gesturing to my video camera.

To the unaided ear, able to extract the remarkable from the weave of usual summer sounds, this serenade could not be more plain, and would have made the two-hundred-and-thirty-mile drive worthwhile by itself. But my camera's mic picks up way too much foreground, too much buffeting breeze and trilling finches, so that the soaring background voices in the forest, when I play the footage back the next day, are vanishingly faint.

This acoustical visitation feels generous and primes us, of course, for the night ahead, but after we eat—Jerry's mother fixes us a pasta dinner—and find our flashlit way back down to camp, the show is over. Jerry sits up by himself for a couple hours, hearing nothing, then he listens while I sleep, sedated by his mom's Italian sausage. Once, at 4:15, he hears possible footsteps, but not clear enough to wake me.

They must be off tending to other business.

Over breakfast, before I head back home to Vermont, he reminds me of another of his favorite axioms, what he uses to keep himself humble. "They don't need us."

Snowy December, six months later, and I've come to visit Jerry again. We reach his spot in the woods at four in the afternoon, just dusk. Since I was last here, he's constructed an impressive hut out of trees and branches, leaves, mud, and moss. We start a fire and try to get warm; it's sixteen degrees, and we huddle on a log seat, drink coffee from a thermos.

In a while, we take a short walk up a logging road. The snow is a foot deep and the night is perfectly still. Jerry makes soft whoops, and we listen. The best wood knock I've ever heard greets us, and we slap gloves in celebration. I'd estimate it's a hundred and fifty feet away, but given the prime acoustical conditions, it comes to our ears clean and immediate, THWACK, but without much heft behind it. More like THWACK, then, but definitely all caps, unmistakable. It's like hearing a word in deep space, such an affirmation of our being way out here at all.

"Look how smart these guys are," Jerry says. "They just have to make a little knock here and there and they know where everyone is. That's their radar."

Fifteen minutes later, on a second exploratory foray up the hill, we hear another reassuring wooden smack, even closer.

"How come it's such a dainty knock?" I ask.

"That's what they do. They don't want no one to know they're here. Last winter, that's all I heard, 'cause the one would be here, and one would be over there, and they'd be going back and forth. And a light knock like that here and there. 'Cause these guys are so smart, they know what to do. They're pros at it."

Back in the hut, Jerry whoops, and not thirty seconds later we hear a series of three knocks from the third-of-a-mile range, quieter than the first but only thanks to distance, obviously more powerful at the source: BOOM-BOOM-[pause]-BOOM!

Delighted, Jerry emphasizes, "That's right after I whooped. And that's right in the swamp, and no one goes back in the swamp. See, that's the kind of knocks I'd get last summer. Three in a row…fifteen seconds…three in a row."

After an hour of shivering, banking the fire with twigs, we tap free of snow, and we hear a branch snap not fifty feet behind the hut. We're bowled over. It's not possible that a deer, say, has *stepped* on the branch, because of the muffling layer of snow. It's a branch snapped up in pure air, by something with sure hands, as can be readily discerned from the audio recording.

Even though we return at sunrise (twelve degrees!) and do our best to draw them in again, that snap is our closest pass, and of course it makes perfect sense that they'd keep their distance, not show themselves by daylight or approach any nearer at night, given how radically Jerry's breaking his normal routine, feeding a whole new person, an unknown man, into the mix. Men hunt. And two men are, from a strategic point of view, much more than twice as hard to deal with than one man. It becomes a group-on-group situation and injects a major new level of concern—the possibility of being triangulated or flanked.

Back in August, as he entered the area one day, Jerry found himself trailed by the one he calls "Dude," an adolescent male, six or seven feet tall but still dwarfed by "Buddy." Arriving at the hut, Jerry said, "Hey… there…Dude" as he slowly brought the camera up to his eye and snapped a shot. It's an extremely low-resolution image, but it does show the figure leaning out from behind a tree at approximately two hundred and fifty feet. It's the sort of picture that wouldn't convince anyone who hadn't come to know, and finally trust, the context of these encounters.

All during our mini-expedition, which is entirely satisfying if not Earth-shaking, I am suffused also with the experiences he has conveyed through his emails, this past summer and autumn.

July 8th, 2007: "I had a great time out there today. I whooped in the field on my way in. As soon as I got in the woods I was being followed. It's hard to explain. We were making our ways to our normal spots where we check each other out. When I would stop walking he would too. When I got to my hut I could see someone was playing out there. Well I heard him getting damn close behind me so I looked and there he was concentrating on his next move, ha. I caught him. He looked right at me right away. Shit man it's been about eight or nine months since we gazed into each other's eyes directly since we met. And he was fuckin' close, like three hundred feet away no more than that. And it was Buddy himself crouched down low like when we met. I got a good look at his feet and can see how he leaves twenty-eight-inch tracks. He is *huge*. He has a gorilla head just a lot bigger than one from Africa.

"We stared each other down. I could hear what he was thinking: Oh shit I got too close. With wide eyes and an open mouth he was dumfounded. So I started to talk like a baby real sweet-like ya know. So he wouldn't feel scared to be that close. I turned to take a pee and out of the corner of my eye he took off in a rush so he's still very nervous of me. I can respect that big-time, this will take time like I thought. When he took off he took a few steps and looked to see what I was up to and before ya know it he was in full stride and gone out of sight quick. Man they can blend in good out there."

September 14th, 2007: "Today though there was an honest effort on his behalf to make contact. I was surrounded by like six of them within a half mile, all around me, with caveman talk and a nice three-minute-long set of knocks and some light vocals behind me to mimic my babytalk, that was Moma I think. And running through the woods.

"It happened, they finally made the next step to friendship. Buddy was happy, I could feel it, a feeling of excitement all around me today. Maybe there's a new baby. I knew who I was looking at today right away. One look and it was Buddy. Huge! He's done this to me a lot, follow me in like that. If you recall I've brought this scenario up before. But we've made a good step today. They might want to speed this up a bit before winter for their own reasons, Hey. So I'll know what kind of eats they like, right? I think the quick change in weather has brought this new approach on maybe. Once they figure out what a PBJ is we're set. I'll bring one out next time

"He left a gift today, a walking stick in the trail like he's done for me before. The hut was tampered with but not messed up, like a passing-through inspection. The candle was moved to the other side of the rock and a few other things were moved too. I could tell it was him, Bud, because it was like he flipped it around with his fingers.

"I also thought I heard a baby Squatch out there today with Mama. It didn't cry just a whimper once in a while, I was right about my hunch of the baby. That's probably why they were happy today they probably just started bringing out the baby. That's why they were on that secluded hill a mile away. They need food. I'll bring a food gift next time. For Mama. I'll have to make a separate area instead of my hut but in view of it for the food to be offered at. Soon enough the leaves will be gone.

October 25th, 2008: "I've been getting little whaah's from the new addition, my friend, and Mama's been trying to shush up this one I can hear. I believe I did as good as I did today because I didn't have my camera, it wasn't charged in time before I left. I played some METALLICA for them. They liked it a lot. I guess that's what I'll name the baby, METALLICA. They really can do good human vocals. It was like a celebration in the woods."

[Author's Note: See YouTube: "Visiting Jerry: Upstate New York Habituation Site."]

5. Texas #1

This is a family of six. The parents are in their forties, with two grown children and, still living at home, a thirteen-year-old son and their daughter Rachel, who is fifteen. The first speaker is the mother.

Since 1982

Things have been happening here for twenty-six years. I think the first episode I remember is being out late one night (about 10:30), feeding some dogs I had in a pen out behind the house. I was by myself and it was dark. I believe the weather was a little on the cool side so maybe it was in the fall. Anyway, as I started to open the gate to give the dogs food, I heard a really low growl and then teeth clicking together. I've always lived in the country, so really I'm not afraid of being outside after dark by myself. In fact we grew up playing outside all the time till the early hours of the morning.

But these teeth sounds were close and very loud. It scared me. It scared me a lot! I didn't recognize the sounds and had never heard them before, so I just dropped the food and walked very quickly to the house.

Over the years we've had some things disappear as well as heard strange sounds in the woods. We never really thought much about it, though. Until Rachel came in one day saying she had seen a bear. As she described what she saw, I was thinking it sounded like a Bigfoot but was a little skeptical. I'd never really believed one way or another. Then when I talked to my oldest son, he mentioned he had just seen one walk in front of his truck on his way home late one night.

That's when we started searching out sightings on the Internet and found the BFRO. It's hard to say how frequently things have happened, since we weren't really looking or paying attention to such things. Since we've been watching for signs, we notice things almost daily.

Mostly it's just calls in the woods, but sometimes there are close encounters. They usually show themselves to the younger kids, more than to us grownups. Our daughter is the main one to see them. She's actually seen the mom and twin babies!

If our chronology is accurate, we saw the mom pregnant outside our backdoor early last December. She was huge and we think her giving birth was imminent. Then Rachel saw two babies in our pasture that ran for their momma and they were about the size of a mid-size dog. They ran on all fours, like a chimp runs.

In terms of "gifts," yes we do leave things out for them sometimes. I wouldn't say we do it regularly. Sometimes when Roy [local BFRO Investigator] is here, he brings food for them. We especially leave food for Christmas. They seem to like it. Usually fruit, pancakes and hot dogs.

Rachel shows rabbits. One time, one went missing and a big rock was found in its cage. So, yes they have left things. What's really funny though is Rachel had several rabbits die pretty close together (they die pretty easily), and she got tired of burying them (because the dogs kept digging them back up). So, she left several right in the edge of the woods behind the house. The next morning we found them on our front porch. I think that was a hint, they didn't want them on their front porch.

Roy leaves a bag hanging in the tree over a little ways from our house. The other day they started calling to us and put the bag in the tree right behind our house...like they wanted us to fill it up again.

Rachel said the mom she saw was beautiful. She had very pretty features. Fine features and very feminine.

But she was "zapped" that one day when she was getting close to the babies. The whole time she felt paralyzed, the mom was cooing to her. She said she wanted to respond and talk to her, but was unable to move or say anything. Then when the babies got out of sight the mom turned to walk away. Rachel followed and called to her asking her to please not go. She turned to my daughter, looked at her, and then walked into the corn. (The corn field was full grown at that point in time.)

I sometimes feel like they are better off than we are because it's so simple. They just live to be together. They don't get caught up in the day-to-day struggle of materialistic things we get hung up on.

Are there stick structures around here? Oh yes. In fact, there's basically a village created out of brush and twigs. It's amazing. It has several huts that are very clean. It is our impression that they travel around from place to place within their territory, never staying too long at any one location. From the calls we know that they are all around us.

I hate the groups that want to kill one to prove their existence. What if that was a member of their own family? How would they feel then. They obviously care about one another. They also live in family groups with a mom and dad.

Rachel is the main one to talk to. They seem to actually interact with her. Usually when she's alone out there with the horses. They really like her. I'll let you talk to her. As long as you don't reveal our specifics, it's fine. It's really not so much a matter of our personal privacy as it is *their* privacy. I would feel horrible if something happened to them because I started this whole thing with the BFRO. We just didn't know much about them in the beginning and now we feel like they are neighbors that are friendly, but like their privacy. They seem to be so protective of one another and truthfully, that includes Rachel. They seem to watch over her. In the beginning we kind of feared they might take her as a pet, but now we know they would never hurt her.

It's not strange to any of us, to me, my husband, my daughter or my son. All of us have seen them now. We just wish we could get some good video. We've got three cameras up, but honestly, haven't gotten much. Roy got some good thermal views last year of three watching me and Rachel. It was on a Sunday about two in the afternoon! They are here all times of the day and night with no rhyme or reason for the timing. I mean you can't say, "Well, every Sunday they'll be here," etc. They just show up when they show up. It's just that it's pretty often. I think they feel safe with us because we interact with them through calls and talking. Then we go and leave them alone.

Even a couple of our neighbors know of them and it's common conversation about the big hairy naked people. But they don't seek out encounters and are not outside that much so don't really interact with them. However, the Feet walk across their roof as well. They are always walking on the roof here. Pretty funny. Last night someone was banging on the outside of my bedroom. I didn't get up. But it was pretty loud.

They knock on the wall, they walk on the roof, I think they may have even jumped on our trampoline before. One night I heard them walking on the roof and then a stumble and bang bang bang (like they fell off the roof) and I went running out to check on them and they were already gone.

We live in a junkyard basically and I think it makes the Feet feel safe. They come around all the time. In fact Roy brought someone here about a week ago and they went walking in the woods about this time of day and walked up on a napping adult. It ran off, startled the humans. Pretty funny. Of course, he didn't take his camera, ‘cause he didn't think they'd be out. I keep saying we need to hook up Rachel with a hidden camera and microphone all the time.

From Rachel

I show rabbits. One day I had a show, so I had to get up about 4:30 AM or so and had to go outside to get the rabbits. I had a headlight type thing on my head when I walked outside, the dogs were going crazy and when I looked into the pasture there were four eyes looking back at me, big eyes. I couldn't figure out what it was so I got closer and closer then my dog barked and they both got up and zipped off into the pasture. I shined the light over there, and there were two things laying there. I thought it was maybe a big cat, I couldn’t tell, they had BIG eyes. They were looking all around and looking right at me. I was shining the light on them and they were reflecting back. So I started to walk towards them, and when I did, Zeke nipped one of them, and they both tore off running really fast, so fast I don’t even remember much of what happened. They went straight up under our neighbor’s fence and stood upright and went into the woods, I was like, Oh, that’s what those are. It was two baby Bigfoots. I was shocked!

And I shined the light back on the cornfield, and I could see them running through the corn, and I was like, I’m going to go get a closer look, so I ran up to the fence, and I get within about six or eight feet of the fence, and Mama walks out, puts her hands on the fence and just looks at me. I’d seen her a couple times before. She starts making this humming noise? And I couldn’t move, I was just like stuck there. I was so scared, couldn’t make a noise, couldn’t do anything. I was getting really scared, and then she started making like this cooing noise, and then I wasn’t so scared anymore. I just kind of stared at her for a little bit. And then, she looked at me and turned around and went back in. I said to her, “Wait.” She looked back at me briefly but kept going. I still went ahead and got my rabbits ready and left.

She had a very human face, very pretty. She didn’t have hair on her face either. Black skin, chocolate black. More like charcoal.

But way before that, I was the first in my family to say, "Hey, there are Foots in the woods," and of course no one believed it until my big brother saw one. They have been there all my life, I just didn't know it.

I was walking over to my grandmother's house the first time I saw one, and it was probably about dusk. It came out of the woods from behind the little house and walked upright towards our house. And then it got on all fours and ran back in. And I got all freaked out and went and told my mom, "There's a red bear," and she wouldn't believe anything about it. That was when I was nine or ten.

So, I got really upset because she wouldn't believe me. Then the next time, me and my cousin were outside playing in the dirt, because that's what we do, and something came stomping through the woods, breaking branches, making all kinds of racket, and we saw something big and reddish brown-black, running through over by the little house. We got really freaked out and ran inside, and were like, "The bear's back." And she still wouldn't believe us.

And so then, like a week later, my big brother was coming down [route name] right over there, and something ran out in front of the car, and he told my mom, "It looked like a bear but I think it was Bigfoot." And then she put two and two together…and *then* she believed it.

My brother feels as close to them as I do.

I feel like they are part of my family. They are always there.

In the beginning, it probably took six or eight months, and then I started messing with them. I used to feed them almost every day. I made this…I just put some flour, eggs, and milk and sugar and syrup, and put some sprinkles on it and cooked it, and would put it out there and come back a couple hours later and it would be gone. And I'd have it up so high that nothing else could possibly have gotten to it. Sometimes off the eaves of the little house. Or sometimes I had this huge table that was taller than me, I had to get a ladder and put it up there. It would be gone every time.

I stopped putting food out there, I got too lazy.

Sometimes I'd just look at them and they'd run away, but after a while, I'd look at them and they'd just kind of duck down and stay there. If I talked to them, they wouldn't really say anything back, they'd just kind of go lower. If I got closer they'd run away. But if it was after dark you could see their eyes.

They leave me stones sometimes, and they whistle at me all the time. And they imitate my mom and say "Rachel" all the time. They will act like they are my dogs crying far away and as soon as I get far-far away looking for the dog they say "Rachel" back at the house, my mom's voice. Then when I get to the house my mom's not home, then they make the dog noise again, making me run back over and over till I give up.

Just the other night, someone was mimicking my little brother calling for the dog. We hear that a lot.

Or they take stuff and hide it and when I go to get it they try to scare me but it doesn't work.

The big male isn't friendly but he is only around sometimes and yes he does do the [infrasound] noise thing to me. He does not like me anywhere off the yard. He sometimes throws rocks beside me but not hitting me though.

Back to the Mother

Lots of activity recently. The other night one actually waved to us. It was midnight, but bright moon. It was probably one hundred yards away. We've watched each other from that close before and even whistled or called to each other, but that's the first time they actually waved back. We were pretty excited. We try not to push any situation to a point where they feel uncomfortable. So after we called to them and waved a couple of times, we went in. We're trying to show them that we know they're there and we aren't trying to hurt them. We're non-confrontational. I think that's why they came to our house when the helicopters were pursuing them in the woods that night.

We've been having helicopters flying low over the woods at night, usually late, and sometimes people flushing them towards our house from the back of the woods. We've found lots of evidence that someone has been trying to find them.

As soon as we can cough up some extra money, we're going to put up more cameras and get another DVR. We have one now with three cameras up. But, frankly, I haven't had time to watch it lately. I need to try to get that done.

Just last night, I was watching Rachel run to Grandma’s, when I saw one at the “little house.” It was sort of pacing and watching me. They often hang around the little house and watch us go back and forth to Grandma’s.

My husband's grandmother lives next door. We live in the country so next door is about a hundred and fifty yards from us. The little house is also about one hundred and fifty yards southeast of us. It’s pretty much just a separate bedroom set away from Grandma’s house. She got mad at Grandpa about something one time and made him build it for her as a retreat. Anyway, after Grandpa died, Grandma has been too scared to stay alone. Rachel and/or her brother have been spending the night there most every night since that time. The kids wait until as late as possible to go. We pretty much have a timeline of 10-12 pm when one of them runs across. I usually either walk them or watch them from the fence that runs in between our two properties.

The Feet usually hang out around the little house for the nightly "show" of us running across and playing in the pasture. We often see one run around the little house when we walk out to the fence. Sometimes they call, but most of the time they just watch.

Grandma has heard things and thinks people knock on her house and walk on her roof. She does not believe it is a Foot. We actually spoke of it to her once, but she didn't believe it. Her memory is not that great, so she doesn't remember any of us talking about it. We don't bring it up.

I get excited any time I see them; however, we do see them a lot. My younger son really likes to see them. He comes running in to get me. For me, it's always at night. During daylight hours, they only show themselves to the kids.

Visting the Family

November 10th and 11th, 2008, I am taken in warmly by this family, the parents and their two children, fifteen-year-old Rachel and her thirteen-year-old brother, whom I'll call Mowgli, because he tends not to wear shoes outside, running through pastures and woods. These are bright, handsome teenagers, only too eager to share their experiences with me.

In fact, both kids go barefoot this afternoon, and so do I, as we cross a vast cornfield. The stalks have been cut and ploughed under, so what's left is a wet mudflat probably two-thirds of a mile from tree line to tree line. Shoes or boots would be sucked off immediately; our feet sink six inches each slimy step.

Rachel's leading us to "the village," a site famous within the family, a sylvan spot where "the Foots" have sculpted huts out of bushes and low trees, bending and weaving them together into a fine mesh, half a dozen green domes with small entrances down by the ground. I've seen pictures.

"I used to come here in the summer, sit in the huts with my friends. It's so peaceful inside there. I went maybe twenty times." It takes her a while to pinpoint the location, though, because things here have been changed around dramatically; the village is largely destroyed, leaving just a few tattered remnants of the former structures. Rachel is saddened, thinks maybe she visited too much, making the outpost no longer so desirable.

In case they've rebuilt somewhere nearby, we poke around. And sure enough, after fifteen minutes, Mowgli finds a large structure, a sort of "blind" that one can walk into, sit inside on a matted floor that he pronounces "really comfy." This place is formed, up top, by a thick tree that's been obviously broken and bent back downward at a forty-five-degree angle to the earth. The resulting screen of leaves and branches has been augmented by many vines and further branches, stuck and twisted in. And it makes for a peculiar phenomenon, just like the "one-way mirror" effect Ammi noted in North Carolina, where she could see nothing past the wall of foliage at the edge of her backyard, whereas when she'd enter the brush, her own home and grounds are very plainly visible.

Mowgli and I stand inside and watch Rachel's red shirt, moving. "Can you see us?"

"Not at all!"

We exit, she enters, and promptly vanishes, confirming, "I can see you both!" Back at the house, thoroughly mud-covered, we survey the two dozen cages, stacked in rows, now standing empty, many of them badly busted.

"They took some rabbits," Rachel tells me, "and they broke some rabbits' backs."

"Didn't that piss you off!?"

"Oh, I knew they didn't mean anything *by* it. Sometimes, they'd just move them around. And the rabbits are really sensitive. Like even if I were to hold them and make a loud noise, they'd have a heart attack and die. So something that big coming through and opening the cages and moving them around…they'd either have a heart attack and die or they'd be put in too roughly and get broken backs and die."

"Why'd they do it?"

"They did it because they watched me moving the rabbits around. I knew they were watching me. I could see them sometimes watching me. I'd go out and take care of the rabbits every day. And I'd move them around or whatnot, make sure everybody was where they were supposed to be. And then eventually they started moving them around, or trying to. The cages would be all smashed up. One time, I found a live cardinal in a cage. When I opened it, he flew away."

That night, over coffee in the kitchen, she fills me in on some background I haven't heard.

"I was out taking care of my rabbits, one evening, and I glanced back at the wood pile. There was one sitting with his back up against the wood pile, and he had his leg crossed over. I watched him and he watched me. I just stared at him for a long time. He just sat there. He had a gorilla-looking face, definitely. I ran in to go get a flashlight and by the time I got back he was gone."

Her mother joins us. "Remember," she asks her daughter, "that one night we were sitting out in the yard, and having a cookout, and they were hollering and whooping, from the north of us, the south, east and west?"

"Mmmm hmmmm."

"That was early on in us discovering things about them. We were having a lot of cookouts, and they'd be talking to us. We'd whistle and they'd talk back, whistling and whooping."

"We were sitting there on the yard that night and we could see their eyes shining in the trees."

"Green and yellow eyes..."

"And blue…"

"And one night," her mother recalls, "we were sitting watching TV, and we heard somebody running across the roof, Boom Boom Boom, and then it sounded like they fell—CRASH! And then you could hear them roll down the roof and hit the ground. But by the time we got outside, they were gone. They ran around up there more than once, but we've only heard them fall that once."

"Was it funny?" I ask.

"Yeah, we were laughing! Somebody fell!"

She goes on to tell me about a spy-structure that appeared, over a few weeks, at the back of their property. "They watch the kids on the trampoline, they sit back there. They made a bench, where there's wood in front so they can see through it, and it's tall, and they sit on it, and they can watch the kids at the house. They made an actual bench. They moved the wood around, piled it up. An observation post!"

Also, the next morning, before I have to leave, to visit Texas #2, Rachel shows me where, in her room, they used to come and pop the plastic cover off the doggie door, and tap on her window, in the lower right-hand corner. She imitates with her fingernails…tap tap tap tap.

"Trying to wake me up, trying to get some reaction out of me. And they'd smack the wall, too, right here. Late at night."

"Would it make you feel good, like, Oh, my friends are back?"

"No! I'm like, I'm sleeping, leave me alone!"

[Author's Note: Since my last visit, researcher Bob Truskowski has spent hundreds of hours at this location, and has obtained high-quality audio, including Sasquatch calls and "chatter." You can hear many excellent clips at SasquatchSounds.com.]

6. Texas #2

This site is one hundred and three miles from Texas #1, but the two families have never met, or communicated, as of the time of these testimonials. The speaker is fifty-four years old. She was chemically poisoned at work in 1993, and has since been on disability. She currently lives alone in a "flimsy lap-siding house," though in the 1990s she shared the small house with a husband and four teenage daughters. Before she moved back here in late 2007, the structure had stood vacant for five years. Her property and the few properties nearby are surrounded by thousands of acres of uninterrupted forest. Less than twenty miles away is the Sabine River Basin, source of hundreds of Sasquatch sightings since the 1950s. On November 8, 2008, I obtained thermal video footage of a Sasquatch in her backyard; see YouTube: "Woodpile Sasquatch."

The Late 1990s

When Bill had the rock fight, we never could figure out who he'd had the rock fight *with,* so we just kind of dismissed it, and after a period of time it just goes into the non-thinking part of the brain. This was in 1998. It was dark out there, there was really no moon, and that area is covered by trees. What he saw was built much like my little spindly daughter. I think it started out as he thought maybe she just chunked a rock at him and inadvertently hit him, but it pissed him off. And so he just reached down and grabbed up a rock and flung one back at her, and hit her, what he thought was her. It made a sound like someone getting their wind knocked out.

Well then they got into this rock fight, and he said it was quick, very agile, in the dark, which he didn't really understand how she could see where she was going because it was so damn dark. And being on the run and side-arming rocks and just beaning him time after time. I was able to look at him later and there were like nine spots on him, because when he'd see the arm move then he'd turn his back to it and it'd get him right in the middle of his back. He must've had eight or nine big ole knots in his back, and a couple on the back of his head, and one on his forehead.

Well, he came inside and he was loaded for bear. He was waiting for her to come in and I said, "What's going on?" and he said, "I'm waiting...just never mind." Then I said, "Well, what's going on?" "I'm waiting on Allison," he said. I called, "Allison," and she comes in from the bedroom, and no of course she wasn't dressed all in black like Ninja Child.

At first he started shaking and then he turned white as a sheet, and I thought it was from getting beaned in the head, like he was going into shock. I thought he'd run into a tree, because he didn't tell me he'd gotten in a rock fight right away, all I knew was he had a big ole knot on his head. But then when I started looking at him, you know, you could see a knot on the back of his head, too. It wasn't till after the kids settled down for the night and we were laying in bed, and I said, "You wanna talk about it?" And he said, "Not really." And I said, "Bill, *what's* going on?" And he said, "Allison never left the bedroom?" And I said, "Bill, she's been working on that school paper all evening." And he said, "I got in a rock fight." And I said, "With who?" And he said, "Well, I thought it was with Allison." I said, "Well, who was it?" And he said, "I don't know, and I don't wanna talk about it anymore. I finally got tired of the rock-throwing, I was just gonna chase her down and whoop her butt." And he chased her down into the ravine and he couldn't figure out how she got down there so dang fast. And where she went.

I think they've been here all along. You know, with four teenage girls, and two of them crawling in and out windows and smoking marijuana, and sleeping with boys (those were *his* two), I was trying to hold down the fort with that, and I was still recovering from being chemical poisoned, and then we had forty heads of milk goat and sixty chickens and thirteen hogs that we were raising from babies and, you know, there was plenty to keep my mind going and my body tired.

So there were a lot of things I would dismiss. Things being moved outside. I'd leave a hoe right there leaning against a tree near the garden. I'd go out there the next day to finish up and it's not there. And I'd find it out by the goat house hanging in a tree. And I'd think, Haven't y'all got something else to do besides mess with my tools? I wish you girls would just leave shit alone, and so, you know, there was ongoing confusion here. All the time. I would get my flower pots and stuff…you know, when you have gardens you've always got *stuff.* And I put all my flower pots in one area and I'd go back and half of them were gone or moved. Mostly I'd notice it overnight.

Then there was the voice trick. The girls would be at school and I would hear, "Mom!" from the woods. And I'd think, That couldn't be the girls because they're at school. But often, you know, it would be so real I would go and check just to see if maybe they got a ride home from school because they were sick? But we had to sign them out…

Or they'd be at home and come inside: "What do you want?" And I'd say, "What are you talking about?" So you know, these Forest People were imitating me and imitating them. I think they'd just sit up in the trees or whatever and that was their entertainment. *Watch this one, watch this one*. Like a prank.

Back in 1999, my daughter had a teenage girlfriend from Arizona visiting. Allison and Michelle (the guest) played in the woods for hours on end, making dams in the creek, exploring, climbing trees, etc. One evening, just before sunset, they came busting out of the woods running as fast as they could go. I could tell they'd been frightened, but they ran right on past those of us sitting on lawn chairs and hid in the bedroom in the closet. I went in and asked what had happened. Allison told me they got scared and came home...but told me no more about *what* had scared them. I believe it took them a couple of hours to finally open up and tell us that they saw a large bear-type creature come down feet-first out of a tree, land behind a bush, stand up on two feet, then side-step behind a large tree trunk and peek out at them. Allison said that the creature didn't move like a bear, nor did it have any "ears" like one. She said she and Michelle had run out of the woods following the well-used path, and the creature followed them, keeping pace—but through the woods to the side of the path. Once they reached the mowed yard area, the creature stayed behind. The girls refused to go into the woods after that, and wouldn't remain outdoors when the sun started setting. After that time, we teased my daughter about her "big, hairy friend" in the woods. Since none of the rest of us had experienced anything remotely similar, she became the butt of some pretty mean jokes.

From Fall 2007

The house had stood vacant for five years when I decided to move back by myself. During this past summer, I came up more and more often and it must have been about the beginning of October I came up and somebody'd taken a big *crap* in the middle of the living room floor. It was just disgusting. I'm thinking, What has this person been eating? I cleaned it up, scrubbed it with Lysol, scrubbed it with bleach, you know, and the smell still was in here for four days. That's how pungent it was.

Then I went into the bedroom and it looked like somebody had brought in a big section of rolled hay. You know how when they bail rolled hay it's in layers? This was one layer. It was about a foot thick by five foot wide and about eight foot long, and it stank hideously, and I thought people around here are using this as a flop house. But this is what I thought was really bizarre, there was a pile of red surveyors' ribbons and orange surveyors' ribbons and different-colored Christmas ribbons and strings and little pieces of wrapping paper.

When I moved back here, there were twelve windows broken out of the house. Two of them looked like somebody had jumped through them from the inside. The back windows looked like they'd been Kung Fu kicked *out.* And I thought, You know what, that's a lot of wasted energy, you kids just have too much energy. Prior to October, some of the windowpanes were broken but the glass was inside the house. But this glass was broken from the inside and pushed out. In hindsight, it kind of scares me: They know the lay-out of the house, too.

One of the ladies on the habituators' forum said, "You know what, I bet you they decided this was a good place for them to get out of the weather, and they are rather warm-natured…they probably kicked it out for air circulation."

Because the house sat empty for so long they may have thought that I'd left it for them. So there was like a failure to communicate.

I had my first sighting on March 2nd, 2008, about 9:00 am when the dogs started pitching a fit. It pretty well changed my world as I knew it. It's one thing to *hear* about the Bigfoot, it's a whole new world when you actually see one. I got probably a twenty-second viewing of my hairy friend, which was quite enough for a first encounter. I was still shaking two days later when the researchers showed up to take my statement. And, when they found the knuckle print, I had to sit down. It was sort of unrealistic until that point. Once they got the eight-foot-long two-by-four board out and I saw *exactly* how big this guy was, that cinched it—I was ready to put out the "For Sale" sign in the yard. But, I started thinking back about all the times they *could* have harmed us, and obviously didn't—and thought also about some backwoods rednecks moving in here and causing them harm. Well, I just couldn't do it. Both my daughters think I'm absolutely out of my mind to live here by myself, but I don't see either one of them volunteering to stay here with me!

So here's how it went that day. I normally get up rather early, put on coffee and let my small dogs and one coonhound out to relieve their bladders. This morning, being rather cool, I didn't stay out with the dogs, but went back into the house. My other daughter, Hannah, was visiting and was still asleep. The dogs began barking. In an effort to quiet them, I stepped out onto the porch. The Chihuahua and sheltie/rat terrier were in a small pen, the coonhound on a tether. The coonhound, instead of going to the end of her tether, was only about 1/4 of the way extended. The small dogs were penned, but were all looking southward, toward the woods. The dogs had a strange bark, not like seeing a person on the road, or a deer—those barks are familiar. The only way I can describe the barking is that it was rather whiney. I looked in the direction the dogs were watching and was shocked to see a large form. The young growth of pine trees was about three to four foot tall. This form appeared to be twice the height of the pine trees. It was really bulky, with no neck, and blended in with the dappling of the larger trees. It was covered in hair, and the length of the hair on its body was maybe six to eight inches. The hair on its head was slightly shorter, roughly four to six inches. You could call the hair color calico: a mixture of charcoal, gray and brown. Overall, the hair was really messy-looking. I think the shoulders were probably between three and three-and-a-half feet wide.

So I kept looking and questioning myself, and realized I truly was seeing something unusual. I pounded on the side of the house, awakening my daughter to also witness this incident. The large form did not turn right or left, but seemed to be moving slowly but steadily backwards into the cover of the woods. By the time my daughter got outside, the creature had blended into the woods.

Then five days later, she had her own sighting. At 8:00 pm, she decided to drive into town. The house has a long driveway that runs right in front of the pine saplings where I saw the figure. Hannah got into her car and drove down the driveway. At the end of the driveway, her headlight beams lit up what she first thought to be a large tree, or stump, in the middle of the saplings. But then this stump started gently swaying back and forth. She turned on her high beams and saw what she could only describe looking "like the lion's head from the Wizard of Oz."

She called me on her cell phone and backed up her car, trying to get the headlights into position so she could see the thing better. Doing this, she took her eyes off it while shifting into reverse, and lost sight of it. Hannah figures the incident lasted about five seconds. She couldn't see the torso or shoulders, just a head. She said the face was like "earthy colors," marbled black and dark brown. There appeared to be a tuft of hair on the nose, but no hair on the cheeks.

She was too scared to get out of her car or drive away, she was basically frozen. After I and my other daughter came out and calmed her down, she finally left.

The researchers arrived the next morning, and here's what they wrote about what they did and found.

"With the witness standing on her front porch, and with an investigator standing at the sighting location with a pre-marked pole, we were able to determine, based on the witness's recollection, that the subject was approximately eight feet tall.

"As is typical of the ground surrounding a growth of young pine trees in East Texas, the sighting area was covered with a thick and heavy layer of dead grass; and the surrounding floor of the mature pines had a thick layer of pine straw and leaves. We performed a detailed search for trace evidence and after quite some time found a fresh impression on a small gopher mound within the pine saplings that exhibited clear digital impressions. Upon examination, it appeared that the impressions represented a knuckle imprint of a large hand, approximately six and one-half inches in width. A cast was made which verified that there were five digits in the print. The print appeared to have been made within the last twenty-four hours as the area had received rain and snow two days earlier. It is possible that the print correlates with the younger daughter's visual incident."

That was seven weeks ago. Since then, all kinds of other stuff has been going on. I had the house bumped. I have a twelve-year-old coonhound, and something was bothering her because she woke me up out of a sound sleep. She was in the living room, just doing this nasal whistling, and I thought, What in the world is bothering that dog? And about that time something hit the southwest corner of my house so hard the windows vibrated. The only thing I could think of is some sort of livestock got loose, or the house fell off the foundation block, or something's trying to get in. So I got my gun, got my flashlight…because it made me *mad*, you know? So I put the flashlight under my arm, got the pistol, and the dog and I went outside. Nothing was there when I shined my flashlight around, but there's this little wiry flowerbed border that was like six foot and it was all torn up where something looked like it had tripped in it.

Often, right outside my window at night I'll have this loud "AAAA!" sound, like the "a" in cat. It was like they were trying to see how far they could push me. So, of course the ladies on the habituators' forum said, "Just start talking to 'em, when you go outside working in your yard." So I had some tomato plants and I was out there and talking to them, saying, you know, "I'm putting my tomatoes in here…It's been a long time since I've been here and had this garden going…" Just jabbering, you know. When I got done doing that I went and sat down on a glider rocker I had put down right at the end of the driveway with the back of it towards the house. And I sat out there for about fifteen, twenty minutes and then said, "Well, if y'all aren't going to talk to me, I'm just gonna go in the house." I got on the second step of the porch and it sounded like I was transported to the Dallas Zoo, in the primate section. It started out with two "Woo Hoo Hoo Hoo!"—two of them doing that. And then it went to that screeching monkeys do when something's been taken away from them.

I started looking around, and north of my house there were five large shapes moving in the trees. They were from about four-and-a-half foot up to I think eight, judging from the trees they were standing behind. There was a row of four-foot trees in front of them and much taller cedars behind them. That's when they started bird-whistling. And then they were frogs. I was getting these calls from just this one little section of the woods. And it blew my mind. So I just stood out there talking to them and all of a sudden…I'm still in the process of mowing down because the house was vacant for five years. There was some grass that was probably two foot high, and through this grass I can see something about three foot wide coming commando-style towards me in the grass, belly-crawling. All I could think of to say was what I said: "Oh for Heaven sakes, I *see* you." And then it froze. And then it crawled backwards. *Backwards*. And I thought, Oh, that is too creepy.

Meanwhile, they were still whistling and pitching a fit out there across the street in the trees north of my house. And then from *south* of my house there came a bird-whistling so loud it made your eardrums vibrate, so you knew it was no bird on the face of the earth.

A *piercing* whistle, and I looked up and there was one pine tree, about forty foot tall, that was like flapping back and forth, swaying back and forth and the swing was getting bigger and bigger. And about ten foot from the top of it was this wadded-up furry creature. It did not look like a raccoon, and I didn't see a tail. But I cannot honestly say it was a baby Sasquatch. But I'm looking at the tree and thinking, How in the world is that tree getting more and more momentum when the object at the top of it wasn't moving a muscle? Something was moving it from the ground, and the only thing I can figure is it was a baby that had gotten out there where it was too visible, and they wanted to get it back in. It was surreal, and you think, Did I really see that? And I thought, I'm losing my marbles, I am becoming delusional.

When I saw that one up in the tree, it looked like one of those (I think they're called) "burls," a big ole knot that comes out the side of a tree. That's what I thought I was looking at. I didn't know they could climb trees, see that's how ignorant I am of what they're capable of doing. So I went back there later, and where the big knot on the tree had been there was nothing but sky.

May 14, 2008

Recently, my cat DeeDee that I raised from newborn got feline distemper and I ended up having to put her down. Brought her home, wrapped in a towel, put her in a box, carried her out and buried her. The next day, I was in the backyard mowing and I hear my cat call from behind the goat house. DeeDee had a distinct meow, I knew that cat anywhere. And I thought, You sorry bastard, you don't know she's dead. Then I thought, Okay, I'll play along with this, and I went, "DeeDee? DeeDee Kitty," and it did it twice more. Later on, I started thinking that maybe it was making this sound to comfort me, you know like when you see a photograph of someone who's gone?

The other day, I was walking out behind the goat house, in the middle of the afternoon, and I heard from the woods what I thought was a frog at first, except it said very clearly, "No bite. No bite." Really it was like a cross between a frog voice and a person's voice.

Then I suddenly realized, and it made me laugh. See, I'm still trying to follow the advice of the ladies on the habituators' forum, so I've been going out to the edge of the yard and talking to the woods, saying like, "I'm just an old woman living here by myself, I'm not gonna hurt you. I won't bite. See, I don't even have my teeth in." When I was chemical poisoned all the minerals got leached out and my teeth started breaking off below the gum line. So I just went ahead and had them all pulled and got dentures. Now, with all this stress here at the house recently, I've been clamping my jaws so much my gums've gotten bruised. So I don't wear my teeth as much.

Now I've heard this a few other times, too: "No bite. No bite," and I almost feel like they've *named* me it.

June 11th, 2008

Last night, I had to let the coonhound LuLu out to go to the bathroom. She's on a forty-foot rope. And I'm getting ready to go to bed and went out and called to her and she wouldn't come in. And I called her again and she wouldn't come in. So I went off my porch to the south, fifteen foot, and just as I came around the edge of the house I hear this "HUH!" And it was so loud I nearly wet myself. And I said, "Look, I'm just going to get my coonhound and I'm going right back in the house." And I could hear it breathing. It was standing in the shadows. See, the only light I've got here right now is the front porch light, which does not shine on the south side of the house, where it's completely, pitch-black dark. I could hear it breathing as I was shaking, grabbing the rope and bringing Lu in, but Lu was almost like she was frozen. And I don't know if I drug, carried, or how I got her in the house.

It traumatized me. They are bound to know that this type of action instills fear. I go out there and I'm telling them, you know, "I live here by myself, now when you make the loud noises close to my house it scares me. I feel like I'm being *threatened*. When I heard that breathing, all the hair on my body stood up, and my heart was beating so loud in my ears. Had it approached me any closer I think I would have had a coronary. I said, "I think I'm going to go in the house now." And of course I know my voice was just shaking.

June 16th, 2008

Today when I was mowing, mowed the front yard, didn't have a bit of problem till I got on the north side, where I'm trying to push back the growth from the woods and reclaim my yard. And where that one was commando-style coming up through the grass? When I started mowing through there, my heart started pounding. It wasn't because I was thinking about the Ninja guy, no I'm thinking about are there any rocks in here.... All of a sudden I had this unexplainable fear, and I yelled out, "You bastards, you are *not* taking over my property!" And my heart's still pounding, and so I tilted the lawnmower up and ran it into that grass, and whatever it was just *left*. So then I'm going in the back, and I haven't mowed way back by the goat house yet, I'm getting there, but the whole time I am mowing I get hit with like "Essence of Gym Locker #3," and "Ode to Skunk," and the third time smelled like dead body. And after the third time I said, "Look, I know you've got all these acres of woods, all I'm asking for is my *yard*." And I said, "Whether you like it or not, I'm mowing." And the smells quit.

These things...they are agile, they can be vicious...you know, any primate pushed can be vicious. I wish I could get you down here and put you over on the other side of the house and let you experience this. I feel like I'm under siege at night. While I was mowing I was getting assaulted with these odors and my heart's pounding because I know they're close, and I started thinking, What is the *purpose* of them making themselves known. There's bound to be some sort of reason. There's nothing I have that they could want, except knowledge. It's not like they want to live in my house. It's not like they want to borrow my *truck*. If they ever got to know human beings and what we are capable of.... I feel like a guinea pig. *Okay, this makes her anxious, and this makes her feel good, watch her relax*. What would happen if they decided, *You know what, we want to take back this area*? There's really no way to explain it except I almost feel like I'm in a war zone. At night, every single window is covered.

July 11th, 2008, a Phone Conversation between No-Bite and Myself (after midnight)

— I can just barely make him out.

—You mean hearing him or seeing him?

—I'm seeing him. He's hiding his face behind a tree, but he's about two foot on each side of this one-foot tree.

—Is he moving at all, or stock still?

—He's just swaying, with his head right behind the tree. Oh, that is so strange. He's just standing out there behind that tree.

—How far away?

—Forty foot?

[She goes back indoors]

—I'm still shaking. Had you not been on the phone, I would not have gone out there.

—Can you peek out any windows, or are they all just completely blacked out?

—Let me go into the bedroom. I got sheers on there that I can hide behind. I don't see him behind that tree, but that doesn't mean he hasn't moved to another one. Hold on just a second... Okay, I have a half-moon-shaped driveway, and he has moved to the other side of the driveway…

—What's he doing right now?

—They just stand and *look.*

—Behind anything or—

—Behind another tree, but he's not really all that behind it now, it's like half of him is behind it and half of him is not, because I can see where his head is...

—What's the light source? Is it moon or stars?

—The only light I got right now is from the front porch and I can just barely make him out, only because he's swaying. I don't understand why they sway. If they'd hold their asses still they wouldn't be seen so easily.

—I know, but often people say they sway, like gorillas. As though they need to be more intimidating than they already are.

—I'm wondering if it helps their binocular vision.

—That's an idea, yeah.

—He's walking off, he's going toward the south, he's going back over to the pine grove.

—You can see him walking?

—Yeah. It just looks like a leisurely walk, just woop-de-doop, you know.

— Aren't you just amazed that they even exist?

—It's sort of like looking at a gruesome car wreck. You can't take your eyes off of it, but you can't dare look away. I feel intimidated more than anything else. I'm amazed at how graceful they are. When they move out of view it's a glide. You don't see them *step.* It's like they're on tracks, and it blows me away because you can't hear the bastards. They are big, they are hairy, they're everything that nightmares are made of, but they're not imagination anymore—eye-glow, hold on. This one's shorter. All I saw was the eye-glow, in the same area across my driveway. I'm shaking so bad. If I drop the phone I'll grab ya as quick as I can. I don't understand why they're so damn curious. From watching me the months I was here, without anybody here, from Halloween until January 10th, until my daughter moved here. So for all those days, I was here by myself. So what is so damn *fascinating*? I got an epiphany today where it was like, We're losing our spot on the food chain, folks.

—We're probably like a car wreck to them, too. If they have an opportunity, where they don't feel threatened, like in this case, and they can just feast their eyes on a human being in its—

—In its own little habitat, too?

—You're like a zoo to them. If they'd wanted to hurt you, they'd have done it a long time ago.

—Unless they were sizing me up.

—They're probably just playing around with you.

—Well, I *don't like the way they play.* Oh there goes another one. That one was little, though.

—What's he doing?

—He just turbo-charged across the driveway on all fours, and disappeared into the trees. Man, he was *quick.* It's like watching a movie and using the fast-forward button X2.

July 19th, 2008

I've made an all-out effort to repel them.

First, I did a big hunt through the house and scrounged up four cameras, which don't work anymore. I mounted them on all four sides of my house.

Second, I spread chemical crystals, flea and tick repellent, on lots of fire ant mounds and by the edge of my lawn. The ladies on the forum suggested this, because it's worked for them.

And then third, I went around my property line and told them *again* that this is *my place* and that they could have all the miles of woods around here but to leave me my house and yard.

Late yesterday evening I was able to sit on the front porch (porch light on) without heightened anxiety. The coonhound, although alert, was more relaxed. She did not bark or whine even during the period of time she was alone outside, which has not happened for many weeks. Lu was so relaxed while I was outdoors she laid down on her side and even closed her eyes.

Whether the result of walking the property and establishing "boundaries," chemically treating the mounds of fireants in the yard, mounting dummy cameras on the house, or even the beneficial psychological effects of me actually doing something constructive—I slept like a baby last night! Nothing hit the window screens, no vocalizations in the yard, even the dogs and cats appear to be much more relaxed.

Right now, I get the feeling the Ancient Ones (as I like to call them) are a *bit* upset with me. When I talk to the woods, it almost feels I am talking to myself. No longer do they give me a responding wood knock. I feel a bit guilty, but I certainly did enjoy that full night of sleep last night. And I definitely enjoy being able to sit on my front porch without being intimidated.

July 20th, 2008

I think I'm busted. I heard a racket on the south side of the house during the night, and I now have a pile of eight sticks lying right under one of the dummy cameras. The whacking on the side of the house was probably a Foot systematically lobbing sticks at the camera trying to activate it. Most likely they have now either figured out it doesn't work or they're wondering how it works without flashing. Dang! These rascals are smart! I figured with the dummy cameras AND chemically treating the yard so they can't approach the cameras would solve the problem for at least a week or so. It took them EXACTLY TWO DAYS. Guess it's back to the drawing board. I know who the dummy is now!

June 17th, 2009

I came inside from mowing, cooled down, took a bath, and relaxed a bit. Just as the sun was beginning to set, I was talking to [a friend] on the phone and looked back by the goat house–OMG! There was a young BF! It was about 5-5 ½ feet tall, medium build, and even had a neck! I don't know if it realized I spotted it, or if it was in a hurry. It made the distance from the goat house to the road in about two seconds. I was stunned at how fast this creature ran! Now I know how my husband could have mistaken a young BF for Allison during that rock fight. With the exception of how fast and agile the creature was, it was remarkably like Allison in proportion.

June 19th, 2009

This evening, about 6:30, I let the dogs out to run a bit and go to the bathroom. I'd been outside about ten minutes when I heard a squalling baby animal coming from near the back fence. The shortest and easiest route to where the racket was coming from was to head west on [road name]. Initially, I thought a coyote had gotten one of my cats. I ran down the asphalt and got about thirty feet from the back fence when a doe busted out of the woods from behind my property, whirled around to her right and stood staring at the woods where she'd just left. I could still hear the animal squalling in panic/pain, and got within about fifteen feet of the doe before she realized I was there. That should have been a warning to me that it wasn't a coyote, but I was more focused on the cry from the woods.

In hindsight, it sounded much like one of the baby goats we used to have, that's probably why I was intent on rescuing the baby from the jaws of the coyote. The doe spotted me, then spun and headed away from the squalling young one. I guess the predator and then the addition of a human being was too much for her to deal with. One of the chihuahuas ran ahead of me into the woods, then came running back and stood on the road.

I ran into the woods, across the rocky ground covered by dry leaves, making quite a racket as I went. As I got within about twenty feet (still at a dead run) I hollered out as loudly as I could, "HEY!" Well, instead of a coyote scurrying off into the woods, I was met with a very loud, very intimidating AAAAAAAAUUUGGG GGGG GGHHHHHH!" I froze. I was too petrified to move. I was located on ground about three or four feet higher than the creature in the woods. Even at that elevation, the hairy creature was nearly at eye level with me. I could see the top of the head, the left shoulder and a very large muscular left arm. The rest was behind brush. Thankfully, the being in the woods took the still squalling young deer and headed into the ravine. At about twenty feet from where the confrontation occurred, the fawn quit making any noise.

By this time, I realized I had been within just a very few feet of one of the Ancient Ones, and a very large, mature one at that. I was shaking all over, scared half to death, my heart was racing and my most urgent thought was to get my stupid butt away from there before the deer killer changed his mind and came back to thump me.

I got back to the house and had a difficult time climbing the four steps to the front porch I was shaking so badly. I immediately went to the bathroom and threw up, then sat on the porcelain throne and found some relief. It was nearly an hour and a half before I was able to compose myself enough to call [friends on the phone]. The Ancient One in the woods beat a hasty retreat when he/she realized I was not the doe coming back for her fawn, most likely a bit embarrassed that a human had gotten so close. Had it chosen to attack, I would not have been able to even move. [My friend] said that the poor, scared critter was probably still sitting off in the woods shaking and trying to regain composure from such a scary incident. I should be ashamed of myself! [He] didn't seem to think I should worry much about any retaliation. He said just behave as normally as you have in the past, and don't let the big critter get the idea it had scared me. It's possible that if it thought I had gotten intimidated, then it could try it again on me, or even someone else. If I go through the motions of things being usual, then the critter will just be more careful next time it goes hunting and the prey makes a fuss. And, since I didn't keep him from catching and keeping his meal, there was no harm/no foul (so to speak).

I had suspected the ravine area was used for catching prey, but never realized it was used during daylight hours, too. It was getting toward evening, but the sun was still definitely up in the sky, it was basically broad daylight even in the woods. Several weeks ago I recorded the "Whistler" back in the ravine well after dark. The Whistler came steadily up the ravine, accompanied by random wood knocks.

I estimate tonight's hunter to be about eight foot tall. He was dark, kind of a chocolate color, with a semi-peaked head. Not a huge crown like a large gorilla has, about half as large. The hair was between three and four inches long, but longer on the forearm, probably nearly six inches. I couldn't tell due to the amount of brush between us (thank GOD) whether it was male or female. To be honest, it didn't matter! I was just very thankful to still be alive. I didn't notice any odor, either.

Now it's almost 11:30 pm, nearly five hours since the encounter. I'm still a bit shaken, but thanks to the calm conversation with friends, I'm doing much better. I have learned another valuable lesson, and survived to tell others. Or, I dodged another bullet, depending on how you look at it.

June 29th, 2009

The only "retaliation" I have received was finding all my lawn chairs in the far backyard. I laughed, brought the five chairs back to the front. The next night, the chairs in addition to some of my flower pots and all four of my antique milk cans were moved to the far backyard. Again I laughed, but said, "Okay, that should make us even now because it is harder for me to move all this stuff back to where it belongs than it was for you to bring it here." I haven't had anything else relocated.

I have to admit, this new reality I'm living is an entirely new world, much like Alice in Wonderland where nothing is what it seems. Could the Ancient One world be similar to our world where there are "civilized" AOs and some AOs a bit wild and opportunistic? My thinking is: There are many more AOs than ever estimated by humans. These beings don't exactly put out mailboxes or construct houses. If women were being attacked by these beings, I truly believe it would be on the Internet. I believe in my heart these are a society and culture that is very well disciplined. It would not surprise me at all to find out these beings are much more civilized than we hairless human beings are. I have no fear at all of being raped or pillaged when I'm out alone. Even when I first "discovered" them, my fear was more of being the main course of their dinner...definitely not sexual entertainment. For some reason, it is the men who seem fixated on this aspect of the AO interaction. I think these men are missing the whole point. I believe with all my heart that the interaction has much deeper spiritual implications.

The government does not want to admit these creatures/beings exist. They'd have to admit they have absolutely no control over their behavior. If forced to "protect" the Bigfoot, then the government would have all sorts of lawsuits requesting restitution for lost livestock, property damage, etc. If it is found this creature is a human-type being, then that poses a whole different hornet's nest. Then they've got this radical society to deal with. These creatures don't wear clothing, don't pay taxes, don't get their children vaccinated, or put them in school. They have not bowed down to the authority of the U.S. government, and I doubt they ever will or could be forced to do so. You know what the government and the settlers did to the Native American Indian. God knows, it was a great effort to wipe them out. And it nearly succeeded. That is what could happen to these beings. By "outing" them [to research organizations that can't be trusted to keep one's location secret], you could be forcing the government to deal with a very delicate problem.

I almost feel I am a "Nazi sympathizer" turning in information on the location and behavior of the Jews. That is how seriously I feel about the information I pass on. The more familiar I become with the Ancient Ones' behavior, vocalizations, social structure and annual "celebrations," the more I feel I am being entrusted with what should be private knowledge. It may be that everyone is not supposed to know they exist. I think those who are drawn to investigate these beings should ask themselves why. Some folks always like a good mystery. Some folks have had a sighting and just want to get all the information possible. And some folks like me are thrust into the center of this whole thing. I don't believe it was an accident.

July 6th, 2009

The Ancient Ones have helped me discover a part of me that was missing. This new reality is quite a bit like going back to childhood and discovering the wonders of the world again. I get to re-look at everything with different eyes. If it weren't for the ladies on the forum, I would never be as far along as I am now, and I am eternally thankful. They helped me to see that the great surge of activity I was experiencing here last spring was not a siege but a celebration, connected in some way with the ancient spring ritual called Beltane, Spring Equinox.

What fun it is to go outside and find yard ornaments rearranged during the night! When I misplace some tool, I can now blame the hairy neighbors rather than my own mind! I am finally discovering joy in my life again, and it's been gone a long, long time. It's satisfying to know about the existence of these beings—and no one else in the area has a clue. It's almost like having a secret life: On the surface I look like your typical old woman, living a meager life, eking out an existence in the middle of nowhere, but if the truth be known, I have a very spiritually fulfilling, adventure-strewn, busy, by no means boring life. Pretty cool!

I don't have a clue why these Ancient Ones have revealed themselves to me, but life would truly be lonesome here otherwise. Yes, I have the four dogs and the three cats to keep me company, but nothing compares to a good mystery needing solved. This alter-reality keeps my mind working overtime. I find myself more alert while driving. I tackle plumbing problems myself rather than invite someone over who also might discover my forest secret. And even if they didn't, I don't want the interruption! At night while I'm at the computer, I hear bumping on the rear wall of the house. It's rather comforting to know they are around.

And that is another change I have discovered in myself—I am more observant of the activities and sounds around me. Instead of slogging through my daily projects, when I rest, I look and listen. I watch what the dogs are doing, where they are looking. I look for the cats to see if they are dozing, or if they are on guard and alert, or if they are chasing each other and energetic. I listen to the sounds of the night. I used to be so closed up to these simple pleasures, now they are mine in abundance. Ancient Ones are amazing mimics. I've heard a brook in my back window—a brook!! I could just imagine a bubbling brook feet outside my kitchen window…what a pleasant thought! Not long ago I heard a cow in my backyard about midnight. There are cows in the area, but close examination the next morning revealed no hoofed creatures back there.

July 19th, 2009

I ran into one of the lady neighbors as I was walking up the road. She asked what I was doing out in the heat, then said, "OHHH! I know—you were looking for Bigfoot signs, weren't you?" I confessed, then she asked where it was I had my initial sighting, and I told her. Okay, she lives about a half mile northeast of me. I asked her if she had looked around her pond and she said, "Oh, we don't have those things around our place. The dogs keep them run off." I just smiled, said I sure hoped so, then went on walking to the house. Folks certainly have funny ideas about where these hairy woods folks stay and where they go.

July 21st, 2009

Well, I just got zapped with infrasound again. I was trying to put a recorder outside the house, on the north steps. Thinking I'd be kind of slick, I acted like I was moving the bowl of cat food away from ants and relocating a window screen (I'm scraping paint off windows). I moved the bowls of cat food successfully, but when I went back to move the window screen it had gotten darker. I turned on the flashlight and a glint of light caught my eye. I was on the north side of the house, facing the west. The glint was to the northwest about forty feet. I used the flashlight and walked toward the light and realized it was a pane of broken glass leaning against the base of a big tree. The pane of glass was about an inch thick, and I was seeing the reflection on the edge of the glass. At this point, I heard the "white-tailed deer bark" about twelve to fifteen feet up the tree I had just illuminated with the flashlight. Knowing this was no deer, but also knowing the AOs rarely attack, I backtracked and picked up the window screen, but for some reason I decided I wanted to peek around to the house. While holding the window screen I used the flashlight to light up a portion of the backyard which is enclosed with fencing. When I did that, I immediately got hit with infrasound.

As I've said, I was familiar with the heart pounding, feeling of fear, heightened anxiety. I heard no accompanying growl or bark, I just felt the pulse of the infrasound. This "pulse" was also picked up on the window screen; I was able to feel it with my fingertips. I decided I had pushed my luck as far as I dared, placed the screen on the steps, and left the area, going back inside the house.

The effects of this session of infrasound so far have lasted about forty-five minutes. I am experiencing nausea, rapid heartbeat, anxiety, fear, tremors and a dull headache. I am still having difficulty typing and collecting my thoughts in a rational, coherent order. The side effects do appear to be subsiding.

August 1st, 2009

I went into the backyard to cut down some fencing. The atmosphere was a bit anxious. I started cutting the wires holding up the gate and got a rock thrown near me. I had come prepared. I said in the most authoritative voice I could muster, "Okay! I just want you to be aware that I have a camera and a digital recorder with me, and I know how to use them!"

I hear this very hesitant voice from across the ravine. "Ummm, lady? Are you okay over there? Do you need some help?" Oh man, I felt like a dingbat… Feeling rather sheepish, I hollered back, "No, I think I've got things under control now, but thanks for the concern!" If the folks in white coats ever question him, I'm sure he'll testify against me.

While I was out there later putting out food for them, [a seventeen-year-old neighbor boy] came by on the road and began with small talk. Then he got to the point of asking what I was putting out the fruit for. I told them, "Well, just about whatever wants it, I guess." I could tell this boy was a bit uncomfortable, so I said, "Young'un, what's eating you?" He said that he'd heard I had Bigfoot on my property, to which I responded, "Kid, they're all over [this part of] Texas. I don't have a corner on the market here." He asked me what he needed to look for to see if they were near his house, so I told him about the tree bends, the X's and the wood knocks. I told him they are not aggressive, but that if you happen to get close to one of their little ones, they use something like a real low growl that we can't hear to make us feel spooked. His eyes lit up and he said, "Oh man! That's what happened that night." And he went on to tell about getting scared when walking home. I told him never to shoot one unless his life absolutely depended on it, because they never travel alone, and getting shot they take real personal.

August 12th, 2009

While I was scraping the overspray off the outside windows, I was able to catch one of the AOs observing me from the brushy area between the house and the county road. I was able to view the being without spooking it off. The reflection in the window wasn't all that good, though, because I had to keep working and vibrating the glass, otherwise I was concerned the AO would catch on to what I was doing. From what I could observe, it was crouched down in a squatting position, the head almost even with the back of the lawn furniture. Even the face had short hair on it. How they can sit there so very still for such a long time is remarkable. If I squatted like that and then had to move quickly, I couldn't do it.

Visiting No-Bite

I arrive on a mild, sunny late afternoon, Texas autumn, and, accepting my gift of genuine Vermont maple syrup, she introduces me around to her two adult cats, two kittens, three Chihuahuas, a sheltie/rat terrier mix, and of course LuLu, the coonhound whom

I'm especially glad to wrestle on the grass—famous, to me, from her role in this woman's arresting accounts.

I'll call her No-Bite, the name her Ancient Ones gave her last spring, after she assured them, "I'm not going to bite you."

We sit out on her lawn, chatting, getting acquainted in person after so much long-distance communication. She's a sweet, kind-faced soul who has been cooking a beef brisket for me all day. As evening descends, one of her neighbors can be heard above us, taking his paraglider up for a spin at several hundred feet.

"Oh, there he goes again. I don't even know who it is, but he's been flying the last couple weeks. Always at dusk."

As the single-person craft approaches, we can hear, from down in the ravine behind her house, five distinct wood knocks, separated by intervals of distance and time. No-Bite's ravine is a lot shallower than mine but still, at two hundred feet deep and a quarter mile long, and filled with brambles, downed trees, bowed saplings, it proves formidable to traverse. Also, the whole affair proceeds slightly uphill, and it's in this direction that the coyote and Sasquatch drive their game—hogs and deer—through. At its outlet, by the road, is where the hunt was interrupted several months ago.

"Hear those knocks?" she says. "They're warning each other to hide, to hunker down. The first time that man flew over, they made a terrible commotion, now it's gotten more subtle." I'm delighted.

After dinner, we sit out in the chill, wrapped in blankets. Indeed, I'm able to spend a total of five nights and days here, and not, for the most part, seeking to gather evidence (like the avid researchers who have visited before, alienating No-Bite with their domineering ways) but rather simply getting a feel for the place, communing with it, exploring the forest and sitting attentive in the yard. Occasionally, at night, we make wood-knock overtures and, I'd say a quarter to a third of the time, either right away or minutes later, receive a crisp response knock from the ravine or from the thick pine forest opposite.

With her permission I do put out my audio recorder, overnights.

Once, hung from the goat house roof, it picks up some light slaps against the walls. The next night at 1:25, set beside a bowl of black plums at the tree line, the mic captures an ear-splitting, high-pitched SMACK! (Hear it at YouTube: "Black Plum Reprimand.") The plums were not taken.

On one of our treks together, No-Bite leads me to a pond within the pine forest that has often seemed the source of middle-of-the-night vocals. The best thing we find here strikes me as a work of art: four separate tree arches all in the same spot, curving elegantly, the ends fed into a thicket of branches and vines. Unlike my own far-northern arches, these cannot be explained away as a by-product of snow and ice build-up; indeed, the farthest tree travels fifteen feet from home to join the others within the thicket. Sorry, skeptics, this just ain't happening without intention, without hands. (See YouTube: "East Texas Tree Bends.")

Another time, she shows me where two long, straight trees have been transported from where they grew, de-limbed, de-barked, and leaned at a steep angle to cross one another twenty feet up in the crook of an ordinary tree. Reminiscent of telephone poles, they're much more reminiscent of the elaborate structure we found on the BFRO expedition in Ohio, 2006, the only difference being that, there, seven trees were thus stripped, raised, and top-crossed.

And then comes the night of the bonfire in the backyard. No-Bite's twenty-year-old daughter and the daughter's best friend are here with us, and we're roasting the hot dogs and marshmallows, having a good time, the two young women acting like kids, giggling and roughhousing.

I leave the firelight and scan the woods with the thermal imager, looking for an upright figure hiding behind a tree, spying on the revelers, its body heat standing out brightly amid the surrounding (cooler) grays. No such luck. But what's that horizontal bar of light, down near the ground, sticking out from behind the debris pile, a perfect vantage point on the bonfire? Should I approach and investigate, camera rolling? Nah, it's probably nothing…

By day, it's clear how close the bonfire was to the wood-pile, about thirty-five feet (picture taken by No-Bite)

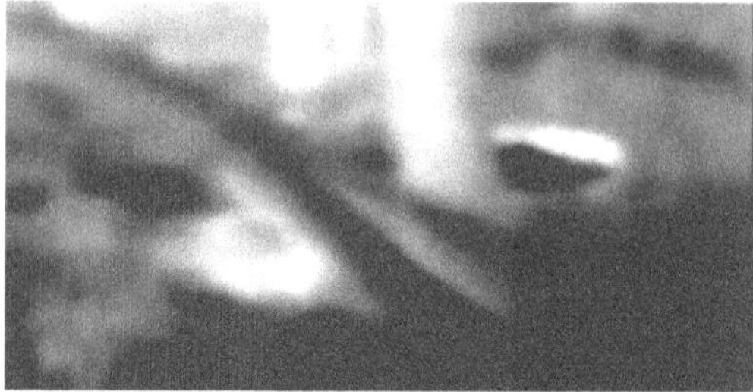

The Sasquatch spied on us through an opening (as indicated below) just eight inches off the ground

The Following Letter was Written by No-Bite to a Member of a Texas Sasquatch Research Group

As I said before, I don't have anything to hide. Right now the trail camera you installed is just sitting out there, I don't know if it has photos or not. Bob, what bothers me about your organization is the mindset that you feel compelled to collect "evidence." If the Ancient Ones want to offer evidence, well that's a whole different ballgame. Right now, I am quite content just to be along for the show.

I've already given you the resources to take this same journey. I've told you how, I've explained what to expect, and that there are no guarantees. I have absolutely no idea why some are accepted, some seem to be chosen, and some folks just sit there and get a numb rear end. It's a strange world out there! And the funny part about it? I laugh now! I haven't laughed like this, this deep belly laughing, in years. I had forgotten what it is like to just cut loose, turn my cares over to a Higher Power and relax. How can you forget how to laugh, a basic human response?

Bob, you know what these people in the woods require of us? Nothing. Not a single thing, they just are reaching out because they desire friendship. The reason I was in awe of [two recent human guests] was they were unafraid of these woolyboogers in the dark. I now know this is because these are people, not woolyboogers. I'm cautious, because I'm still new and also I'm alone here, but I know there is no need to be afraid of the hairy folks here. I just feel so very blessed to have had my eyes opened so I could feel how full my life really is.

I don't care whether science is ever able to prove these people exist. At this point, I have even given up trying to prove to you that I have them here. I don't need proof anymore. Whether or not they are here is so very insignificant when the big picture is considered. I so wanted you to put down your damned game cams, digital cameras, digital recorders, infrared cameras, motion detecting equipment and all the God-blessed stuff you constantly tinker with so that you could experience a whole new dimension in "research." What do I know—I'm just someone who happened to be blessed with seeing these reclusive beings. These aren't "chance sightings," they are deliberate. These are an indigenous people. They have their own laws to be obeyed, their own culture, their own beliefs, and social order. Finding these people in my own backyard is akin to finding gold! I don't want them dissected, photographed and ID'd, fingerprinted, probed and grilled. I feel they are now my extended family, and when folks mess with family, I get angry and protective.

How many others are experiencing the same things? I'm not certain. Maybe (and this is a guess) several thousand around the world. What's happening here is also happening elsewhere. If I was the only one experiencing these situations and seeing these occurrences, I truly would have to wonder about my mental well-being.

There are those on the fringe of this knowledge that so want to be included, but for whatever reason they can't or don't see. Many individuals who are still intent on collecting evidence and documenting sightings quickly back off when the deeper, more meaningful experiences begin to happen. That's why many of the folks who report sightings soon drop off the radar.

The research approach presently used is demeaning and insulting, and that approach has been abandoned for a more person-to-person approach. Just like if you were trying to get to know your next door neighbor. Once these reclusive people realize you know the bluff charges and vocalizations, etc., are basically a hoax, you end up on a fast track to a whole "other world," is the best words I can come up with. The individual has both feet on the ground, but his/her mind becomes open to something that just defies scientific explanation. If you would like to speak with those taking me on this new course, you'll have to get in line behind me—because so far there has been no spoken word. I do know I have to constantly fight back the fear of the unknown and persevere if I want to go further.

You are wanting blood and guts, rock hard evidence of these people. If I did have it, I wouldn't provide it to researchers who want to tag and label. I would absolutely love to think you would drop any preconceived notions and just come and sit and visit, but for whatever reason, God has created you with blinders. Maybe you are not supposed to see what is happening.

Bob, my entire perception of "my world" has changed, and I'm just beginning to understand some of the things going on. The only thing I can compare it to is being mentally reborn. Nearly everything I thought I knew has been given a different slant. Once I dropped what I expected of these people, an entire culture was opened up to me.

Because I was so fearful, these beings spoonfed me a little at a time. What I am able to tell you so far is this: These are a people who do not want to be "found." A few open-minded people around the world have been blessed with the opportunity to step through the established wall these people have built. These people fit in with humans like "gears." What humans lack, these people possess. What these people lack, humans possess. Why is it that more and more individuals are having sightings? Because I believe the walls are coming down between the two cultures, but not completely. At this point I feel it is my purpose to plant the seed within you.

www.ingramcontent.com/pod-product-compliance
Lightning Source LLC
Chambersburg PA
CBHW060356290526
45791CB00002B/529
* 9 7 8 1 4 9 6 0 1 2 2 8 9 *